Modern Crewel Embroidery *for Beginners*

Dedication

To you, my dear reader. I admire your intelligence and curiosity and I do hope this book will give you a well-deserved reward.

Acknowledgements

To my publishers. I am grateful for your support in this very special time of my life. And also for encouraging me to make my embroidery ideas and skills more systematic and well arranged.

Thank you so much to Appletons Wool (www.appletons.org.uk) for your kind help and support.

First published in 2026

Search Press Limited
Wellwood, North Farm Road,
Tunbridge Wells, Kent TN2 3DR

1 2 3 4 5 6 7 8 9 10

Photographs on pages 1, 2, 3, 7, 9, 10, 11, 13, 14, 17, 18(b), 25, 27, 28, 29, 35, 36, 37, 45, 47, 55, 57(t), 59, 67, 68, 69, 71, 79, 80, 81, 89, 90, 91, 92, 93, 99, 101, 102, 103, 104, 105, 111, 112(b), 113, 114 and 115 by Mark Davison; techniques photographs by the author; all other photographs by Alex Popov.

ISBN: 978-1-80092-358-4
ebook ISBN: 978-1-80093-341-5

Bookmarked Hub
Extra copies of the templates are available to download free from the Bookmarked Hub. Search for this book by title or ISBN: the files can be found under 'Book Extras'. Membership of the Bookmarked online community is free: www.bookmarkedhub.com

Publishers' notes
The Publishers and author can accept no responsibility for any consequences arising from the information, advice or instructions given in this publication.

For errata, please visit our website (www.searchpress.com) or the Bookmarked Hub (www.bookmarkedhub.com).

GPSR information can be found at www.searchpress.com
Printed in China, TT052026

Modern Crewel Embroidery *for Beginners*

STEP-BY-STEP TECHNIQUES AND
8 COLOURFUL PROJECTS

TATIANA POPOVA

SEARCH PRESS

CONTENTS

4

5

6

7

8

Introduction

Through centuries, the beautiful art of crewel embroidery has undergone lots of changes; new techniques have been introduced (some historians think the initial crewel only involved four or five stitches). Popular crewel motifs have been altered under the influence of the shapes of exotic tropical plants and fruit drawn on eastern vases and carpets – saying nothing of the rich ornaments of Elizabethan crewel! Yet I am prepared to bet that the change we are witnessing nowadays is the most curious and bizarre: I mean the introduction of new materials for stitching crewel patterns. Until recently, only crewel wool has been used for this. Moreover, the very word 'crewel' means wool. Still, this novelty is quite pardonable, for few can resist the charm of crewel patterns, and also the temptation to try new threads, plentifully available in modern craft shops. Neither can I, and having experienced the joy and pleasure of stitching, I am willing to share it with others – with beginners in crewel embroidery.

Being a beginner has become an ambiguous characteristic: lots of people are inclined to think of a beginner as inferior to a professional, yet, in reality, beginners are zealous, hard-working and diligent. Like inquisitive children, they are ready to make efforts to learn something new. With crewel embroidery it is twice as rewarding, for having mastered a craft, you become capable of creating artworks!

In my opinion, the colour of threads and texture of stitches are the two main attractions of embroidery. No doubt, colour comes first. You will find that areas of your designs tell their own stories or play tunes of their own in the 'joint orchestra' of the finished embroidery. Change the colour – change the tune! Let this encourage you to play with colour, making your thread choice. Stitch selection is a different story. Choosing stitches for this book, I thought of the words of Professor C. S. Lewis: 'If you are trying in a few minutes to tell a man how to get to Edinburgh you will tell him the trains: he can, it is true, get there by boat or by a plane, but you will hardly bring that in'. I chose stitches formed by repetition of a particular simple move of the needle (called the 'Key Move'). Learn it, and you know the stitch. I also took the liberty of 'telling you the trains', and not mentioning variations or alternative stitch names.

You may not want to work each design of this book, but always practise the stitches for the design you have chosen. Never feel guilty for not stitching for a while. Most of us are casual embroiderers: we take up a project every now and then, and enjoy developing it in the way and at the pace we like.

Stay happy in following your creativity!

Tools and materials

Embroidery uses only a few tools and materials. As you become more experienced with this beautiful art, you may wish to add more to your craft box, including the extra items listed over the page.

ESSENTIAL ITEMS

1 Threads

Traditional crewel embroidery is stitched with wool, while a modern approach uses all kinds of threads. The projects in this book use cotton threads, which can be easier for beginners, but you are welcome to try using crewel wool, using the conversion chart on page 15.

You will need one skein or ball of each thread colour to stitch any of the eight projects in the book.

2 Needles

With few exceptions, crewel embroidery is stitched with sharp-pointed needles: size 20, 22, 24 and 26 chenille needles and size 8 or 10 crewel needles (also called 'embroidery needles'). A few techniques in this book also use a size 20 blunt tapestry needle. If possible, choose a gold-plated tapestry needle: a different colour needle makes it easier to spot and you will never mistake it for a sharp needle. I find John James one of the best needle manufacturers, and they offer sets of needles for crewel embroidery.

3 Fabric

It is a good idea to stitch through a two-layer 'sandwich' of fabric. The top one (the embroidery fabric) has the design transferred onto it. The backing fabric underneath helps to support stitches.

Embroidery fabric

I use cotton fabrics of the highest quality I can get, as they are easy to work with. Choose white or lighter colours, and avoid stretchy fabrics at all costs! Fabrics for needlepoint are no good for crewel embroidery: their heavy threads are difficult to stitch through, and Aida cross-stitch fabric has a distinct texture that isn't suitable for crewelwork.

Traditional crewelwork is worked on a fabric called linen twill, which is a heavier fabric (therefore, no backing is needed). As linen twill is more opaque, you may need to use a light box when transferring a design onto it (see page 16).

Backing fabric

Any kind of finer cotton fabric works well. Avoid fabrics that are stretchy as they won't provide enough support for your stitching and may cause contracting of the embroidery fabric. Heavy fabrics are not suitable for backing, as they make it tricky to pass the needle through both layers of fabric.

4 Embroidery hoops

To prevent the fabric from contracting, always use a hoop as you embroider. Whether your hoops are plastic, wooden or bamboo makes no difference, as long as they provide a firm grip on the fabric. The outer hoop should fit tightly to the inner hoop around the whole circumference. I find Nurge one of the best manufacturers of embroidery hoops. Try to use hoops large enough to fit the design you are going to stitch, as moving a hoop around the fabric as you work may impact the quality of the finished embroidery.

5 Scissors

Small, sharp embroidery scissors are essential for cutting threads precisely; curved-blade scissors can be even better. Use any sharp scissors you have in your household to cut fabric.

6 Pencil

Use a 2B pencil to transfer a design onto fabric.

7 Sewing pins

Have a few sharp pins at hand to fix the paper to fabric when tracing a template. Pins may also come in handy as you stitch.

4
1
2
5
7
3
1
6

EXTRA ITEMS

1 Quick-grip bar clamp

It is far more convenient to have both hands available as you stitch. I like working with an Irwin Quick-Grip bar clamp, to attach and unclamp the hoops to/from a tabletop in seconds. You can buy any kind of embroidery hoop stands, yet a quick-grip bar clamp is much cheaper.

2 Thimble

Put a thimble on the tip of the middle finger of your stitching hand, to protect it from being pricked with the needle as you push it through the fabric.

3 Pincushion

Choose a pincushion filled with natural fibres, such as wool or horsehair, to keep needles in place and prevent them from rusting. Another nice filling is emery powder, which will sharpen and polish your needles and pins as you push them into the pincushion.

4 Needle minder

Readily available to buy online or in craft stores, a needle minder consists of two small magnets. Holding one of the magnets over, and the other one under your fabric, attach them to each other. The top magnet usually comes with a small button on the top to hold your needle – a cute way to stop you from losing your needle and a handy place to rest your needle as you trim off the thread tail.

5 Needle threader

If you find threading a needle frustrating, using a simple needle threader can help.

6 Seam ripper

Its sharp point is the safest and easiest way to unpick stitches – hopefully you won't need to use this often!

7 Clear sticky tape

Clear sticky tape can be useful to collect loose fibres from the fabric after you have unpicked stitches.

8 Light box

Useful for transferring designs onto dark or dense fabrics. Pin the template to your fabric, then place both onto the light box to trace the design. If you don't have a light box, you can use a well-lit window for the same purpose, but the light box is more convenient, and your hands won't get tired as you do the tracing.

9 Pens and fabric markers

Instead of using a pencil to transfer a design onto fabric, you could use Sakura Micron pens, numbers 2 or 4. They provide fine and permanent lines, bright enough to contrast with the fabric. Alternatively, you could try using a water-soluble fabric marker (the marks can be dissolved in cold water afterwards). On dark fabrics use a white fabric marker.

10 Fabric scissors

There's no need to buy expensive fabric scissors, as we are not going to use them as often as dressmakers. If you do have them, do not use them for cutting paper, or the sharp blades will be bluntened.

TIP

To keep your work area clean and tidy, use a small box or container for thread trash, so that you do not catch discarded thread on the needle as you stitch.

8

3
10
6
9
5
2
1
4
7

THREADS

Selecting embroidery threads for your projects means choosing thread type and colour.

Thread type

With all the vast variety of threads available today, let us focus on three thread types:

- crewel wool
- pearl cotton
- stranded cotton.

1 Crewel wool

Crewel embroidery is traditionally stitched using crewel wool. Originally this was due to sheep's wool being the only kind of fibre available. A similar thing happened to other embroidery techniques: using particular colours – for example, using black and red for some embroidered towels – was due to there only being two dyes available. Another example: stitching in pure silk ribbon or chenille cords had long remained a privilege of high-class ladies, because of the high cost of those materials, as well as of steel needles.

Following tradition is a great thing, and the variety of colours of crewel wool available today is amazing. The UK's number-one manufacturer of crewel wool is Appletons, and you can trust their threads absolutely!

Modern life offers another approach, the result of centuries of cultural and merchant exchange between countries and nations of different parts of the world. That is, to use the vast array of threads we have available nowadays. Cottons and silks, as well as all kinds of viscose, artificial and metallic threads – and even seed beads – can be used for embellishing those intricate crewelwork patterns.

Follow either the traditional or modern way, or try each of them in turn to see what works best for you.

2 Pearl cotton

Pearl cotton threads are ideal for learning embroidery, and not only for learning – their beautiful finish is irresistible for stitching! Pearl cotton comes in several sizes: the higher the number of a size, the finer the thread. Size 8 tends to be needed most often, a finer size 12 thread is used for fewer cases, and the heavy size 5 is the least common, used for few very particular cases in crewel embroidery. Sizes 8 and 12 come in balls, and size 5 often comes in skeins, as shown to the right. Pearl cotton is indivisible thread. Work with lengths of around 30–50cm (12–20in) for stitching and store pearl cotton in cardboard boxes.

Most of my pearl cotton threads are from DMC. I also love Anchor threads for their vast palette of pearl cotton in size 12, and the shinier finish of their threads.

3 Stranded cotton

Stranded cotton comes in skeins, formed of strands. A strand consists of six fine threads joined together. For most types of stitching you will need one or two of those fine threads. Follow the instructions on page 19 for the only correct way of separating fine threads without tangles and knots.

Though the options for storage of stranded cotton threads are numerous, keeping them loose in a drawer or box seems like the best approach.

If you would like to replace cotton threads with crewel wool, use one or two wool threads for one or two stranded cotton threads, and 3–5 crewel wool threads for pearl cotton. I recommend you do some test stitching first to make sure you like the result.

1

3

2

Thread quality

Hand embroidery, while – no doubt – an enjoyable pastime, takes a lot of our effort. And of course we expect to get something nice as a reward! For this reason, always choose threads you are going to use with care. Threads of well-known brands are of high quality, colourfast, fade-resistant and – in the case of cotton threads – also mercerized (that is, smoother and more lustrous, compared to untreated cotton).

It is true that the price of some off-brand threads may be very tempting. Yet, the price is not a reason for using cheaper threads – and being a beginner embroiderer is not an excuse! Your first steps will not be as enjoyable as they are with high-quality threads, and the results of your stitching may be frustrating. Very cheap threads are not convenient for stitching: they are neither smooth, nor nice looking, and are more likely to bleed, due to the lower-quality dyes used in their manufacturing. Just think: one can hardly expect a fruit salad to taste nice, if one has made it out of unripe fruit.

If you are unsure about the quality of your threads, perform a simple test: cut some thread and wrap it in a small piece of spare white fabric, then hand-wash with soap and let it dry (alternatively, steam iron the 'fabric sandwich'). If no stains of the thread colour appear on the fabric, the threads are colourfast, and if you are happy with their look, use them for stitching without hesitation.

One more point. If, for example, a friend presented you with a box of DMC threads leftovers, and the threads look somewhat worn out due to the improper conditions of storage, use these threads with confidence for your doodle-stitching (to learn new techniques), but purchase new threads to embroider designs.

Let nothing get in the way of the joy of your stitching experience!

Reading a thread label

Balls of thread

Both DMC and Anchor balls of size 8 and 12 pearl cotton thread come with a round label on top of each ball. The labels show the brand name, colour number and thread size (thickness).

DMC pearl cotton thread, sizes 8 and 12.

The three key pieces of information to take from the thread label are: the brand name, thread size and colour number.

Skeins of thread

DMC and Anchor size 5 pearl cotton thread, as well as stranded cotton thread of any brand, comes in skeins, each being supplied with two labels wrapped around them. The narrower label features the brand name. The wider label (with the barcode) shows the colour number. The placement of this wider label is a hint as to where to look for the 'pull thread tail' – see page 19.

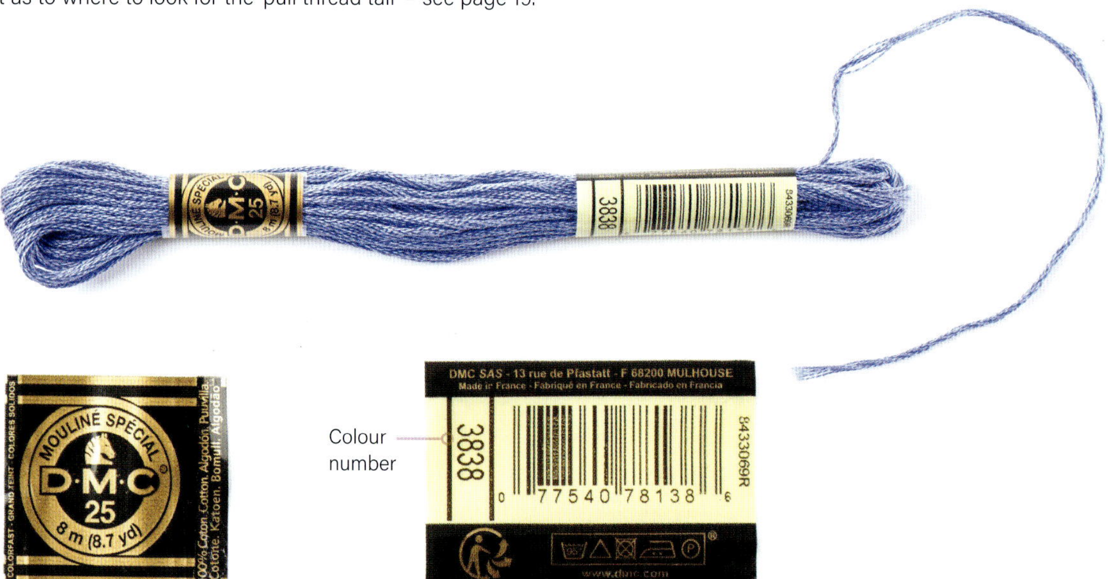

DMC stranded cotton.

Choosing thread colours

Colour is an important factor when designing, and a personal choice. If you like the colours in the projects in the book, you can copy them exactly, following the project instructions. However, if the colours in the designs are not to your taste, you may wish to replace them with some of your favourite shades.

Choosing colours that go well together is both exciting and rewarding. Play with thread skeins or balls: take your thread treasures out of your craft basket and have fun arranging them in different ways! Then take photographs of the colour combinations you like.

Keep in mind the proportions: a combination of the same-size thread skeins may look pretty together, but for the actual embroidery you may want to use more of one colour shade and less of another. To make your embroidery look balanced, repeatedly apply some of the colours for stitching various areas of your design.

Photographs of still life, nature or landscapes are also a nice source of inspiration for choosing a colour. Take advantage of what you see around you: a piece of fabric, a colourful pattern on a cup or a plate, some wallpaper, or even a leaflet or business card – you never know what trifling thing may catch your eye when you are seeking a fresh colour combination.

And always remember there are no 'right' or 'wrong' decisions about colours. If you like your colour combinations, go ahead and enjoy your embroidery!

DMC to Appletons conversion chart

DMC	Appletons	DMC	Appletons
B5200	991b	760	143
Ecru	988	761	753
208	894	772	847
211	891	778	711
225	621	794	821
309	227	814	716
311	326	815	305
315	528	816	148
320	644	822	791a
351	124	828	562
352	204	830	336
353	622	841	931
368	402	842	982
369	541	890	835
415	963	902	716
444	312	913	524
501	156	931	323
502	155	938	338
503	643	945	762
517	566	959	463
518	565	987	403
519	462	988	424
522	965	989	402
554	451	3022	965
561	157	3033	971
640	967	3045	343
642	965	3053	154
646	966	3078	872
647	924	3345	256
666	995	3346	426
676	902	3348	401
712	881	3705	502
725	312	3753	561
727	842	3756	991b
733	242	3760	486
738	762	3765	489
739	761	3787	968
741	476	3813	524
742	475	3822	902
743	694	3823	331a
744	842	3842	488
745	851	3865	991b
746	881		

Getting started

The best approach in mastering embroidery is to learn the stitch techniques before you start on your first design. Of course, you may not want to embroider all the designs in this book; but whichever your choice, start by practising the stitches. There are few things needed before you begin either doodle-stitching or embroidering a pattern: you just need to adjust the hoops and pick up needles and threads.

ADJUSTING THE HOOPS

Whether you are going to practise stitches or embroider a design, hooping the fabric is a must.

1 Preparation

Choose the appropriate size of embroidery hoop, that is, the diameter of the hoop must be at least 1cm (½in) wider than the design you are going to work. For practising stitches, the size of hoop does not matter.

Cut a piece of embroidery fabric which is 10cm (4in) bigger each way than the diameter of your hoop. Cut a piece of backing fabric around the same size as the embroidery fabric.

Spray the embroidery fabric with water and iron it until dry. This will remove creases and pre-shrink the fabric. Do the same to the backing fabric.

2 Transferring a design onto embroidery fabric

If you are going to practise stitches, skip this step.

Photocopy or print onto plain paper the template for the design you are going to stitch (for the designs in this book, use the full-size templates on pages 120–127). Place the template onto a table or flat surface. Take the ironed piece of embroidery fabric (the backing fabric is not needed for this step) – have a look at both sides of the embroidery fabric and decide which of the two looks nicer to you – this will be the right side. Lay the fabric over the template, the right side facing up. Centre your design underneath the fabric and attach it to the fabric with sewing pins – one on each corner of the paper.

Check whether the fabric is transparent enough for you to see all the details of the template. If it is, trace the outlines using either a Micron Sakura pen or a 2B pencil.

If you cannot see all the lines of the template clearly, you will need to use a light box or well-lit window for tracing. Switch on the light box, place the template (pinned to the fabric) on the lit surface and trace the design. The disadvantage of using a window is that the surface is vertical and your hands may get tired while tracing, but you might find it easier if you attach the template to the window with masking tape.

3 Loading the fabric

The step photographs below show the plain embroidery fabric, with no design transferred onto it. This is to stress the point that for practising stitches you also need to hoop the fabric.

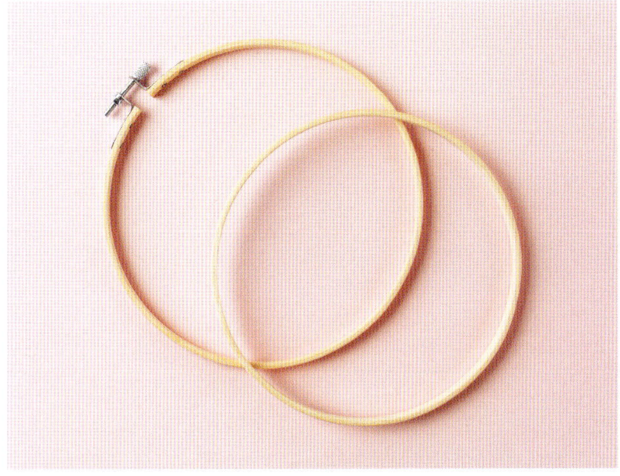

1 Unscrew the hoops, separating them into two pieces. The outer hoop has a closure attached to it, and the inner hoop is plain.

2 Place the inner hoop on a flat surface. Place the backing fabric (cream coloured in the photograph) on top of the inner hoop. Place the embroidery fabric (shown in white above) over the backing fabric, right side facing up. (The photograph shows the fabrics folded, to make the hoops visible for clarity.)

3 Take the outer hoop and unscrew its closure a little more to allow space for the fabric. Pop the outer hoop over the fabric and inner hoop. Loosely close the screw.

4 Gently pull the fabric outwards and down, working around the hoop. The aim is to stretch the fabric almost drum-tight, so if it gets visibly loose as you press your hand against its centre, the fabric needs more tightening. Work around the hoop again, and give the fabric a really good tug. Now fully tighten the closure.

CHOOSING THE NEEDLE SIZE

Some needles – for example, crewel and chenille needles – have sharp tips; use these for regular stitching. Some other needles are blunt, like tapestry needles. Use tapestry needles for whipping, weaving or working other stitches detached from the fabric.

Needles come in various sizes, and choosing a suitable size is important. Below is a chart for matching the needle size to your thread.

Keep in mind that this chart is not an absolute guide, due to the difference in the types of fabric we use. Trust your feelings as you bring the needle through the fabric: if you find it somewhat difficult, use a larger needle, otherwise your thread may become fuzzy because of its friction against the fabric and the needle eye. For the best results, your needle should pass smoothly through the fabric when stitching.

THREAD TYPE	NEEDLE SIZE
1 thread of stranded cotton	Size 8 crewel (embroidery) needle
1 or 2 threads of stranded cotton	Size 26 chenille needle
3 or 4 threads of stranded cotton; pearl cotton size 12 or 8	Size 24 or 22 chenille needle Size 24 or 22 tapestry needle
6 threads of stranded cotton; pearl cotton size 8 or 5	Size 20 chenille needle Size 20 tapestry needle

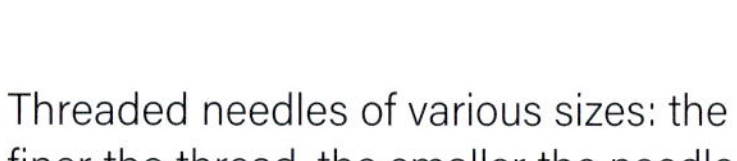

Threaded needles of various sizes: the finer the thread, the smaller the needle.

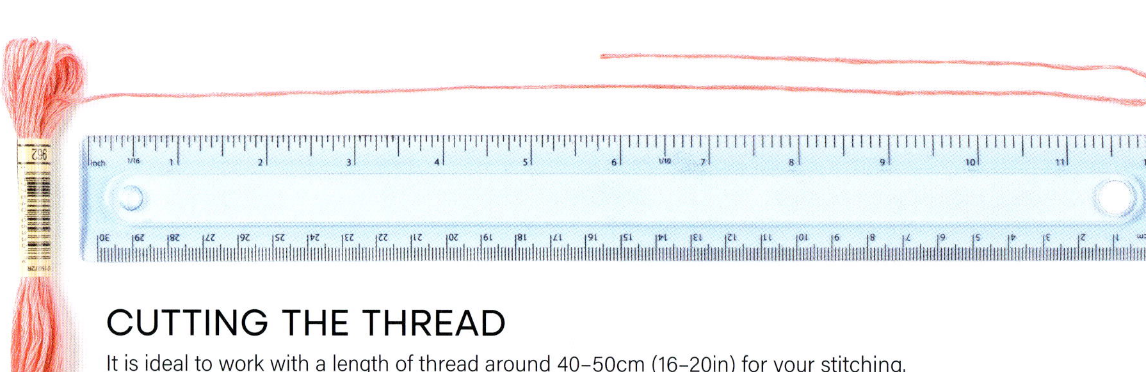

CUTTING THE THREAD

It is ideal to work with a length of thread around 40–50cm (16–20in) for your stitching. While it's tempting to use a longer piece of thread to save time, threads can become dull and fuzzy when repeatedly passed through the fabric, which may ruin the look of a finished stitch. Working with shorter threads is better.

A practical way to cut the right length of thread for stitching without measuring it precisely is to use a handy object of a similar length, such as your forearm or one of your hoops. Hoops may be a little smaller than the required length: make a habit of adding 10–15cm (4–6in) to the hoop diameter.

Separating threads of stranded cotton

Most sizes of pearl cotton thread come in balls. Since they are indivisible, just cut the appropriate length by unwinding the ball. Size 5 pearl cotton comes in skeins, and to get a piece of thread you need to remove labels, untwist the skein, trim away the knot and then remove a single thread.

Stranded cotton thread is divisible, and you often need just one or two threads from within a strand for stitching. See below for how to effectively pull one thread out of a strand. First, cut a strand of around 40cm (16in) long: grab the thread tail which comes from underneath the wider paper label (see page 14), and pull on this tail until the proper length of thread is released. Cut off this loosened strand: it consists of six threads.

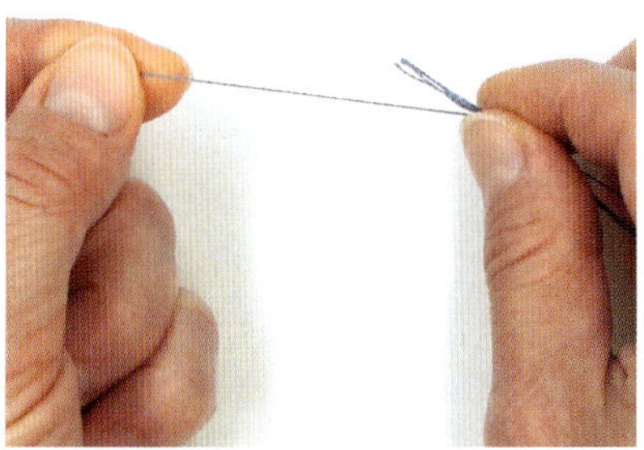

1 Pick up the 40cm (16in) strand, and grab at only one thread.

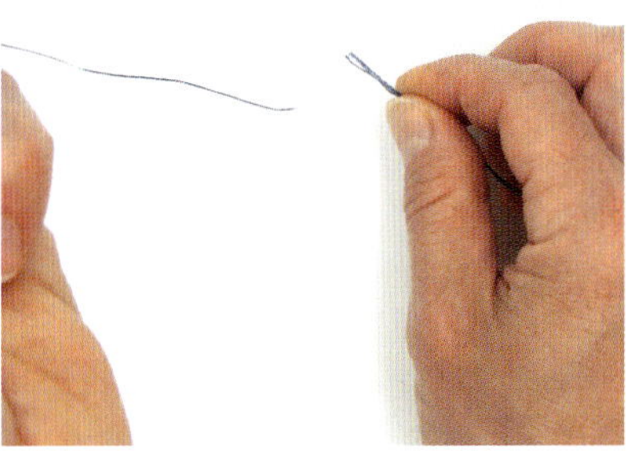

2 Tug on this thread until it comes out. If you need two threads for stitching, repeat the procedure, then, as you thread a needle, bring both threads through the needle eye.

TIP

Do not try to remove two threads in one go, or it will turn the strand into a tangled mass.

Separating threads of size 5 pearl cotton

Most often, size 5 pearl cotton thread comes in skeins. These skeins (also known as hanks) differ from skeins of stranded cotton thread – hence the difference in the way of managing them.

1 Slide both labels off the skein and untwist the skein into a big loop.

2 Find the knot joining two thread tails together. Snip off the knot and cut through the whole skein to open the loop.

3 Cut the strand in two (or even in four). Pull out one thread for your stitching.

THREADING THE NEEDLE

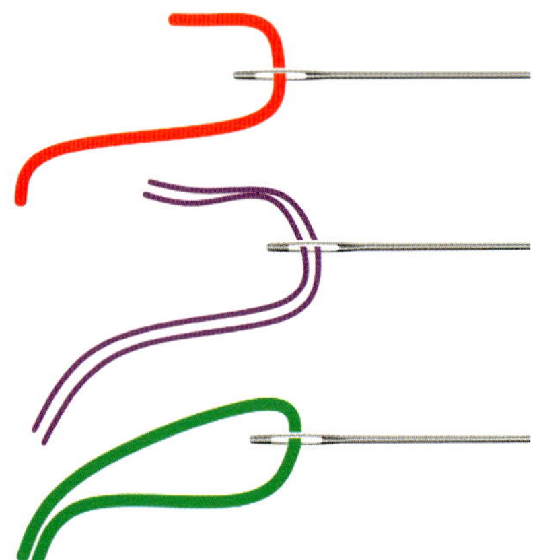

Bring a length of thread through the eye of the needle you have chosen for stitching. If you find threading troublesome, use a needle threader.

Most stitches are worked in a **single thread**: one thread coming through the needle eye (shown in red thread on the right).

Some stitches call for a **double thread**: two threads come through the needle eye (shown in lilac thread on the right).

Very few techniques allow using **bent thread** for stitching (shown in green thread on the right). Unless it is mentioned in the instructions, never use bent thread for stitching, or your work will look untidy.

ADJUSTING THREAD TAILS

Whether using single or double thread, one of the thread tails should be shorter (the anchoring thread tail), the other longer (the loose thread tail).

In years gone by, it was crucial that the reverse of embroidery felt soft, as a good deal of stitching was done to embellish clothes. Nowadays, many embroiderers use knots guilt-free! That is because most of our stitching is turned into wall-hangings with the back safely hidden. Therefore, I recommend you make a regular knot on the anchoring tail of your thread.

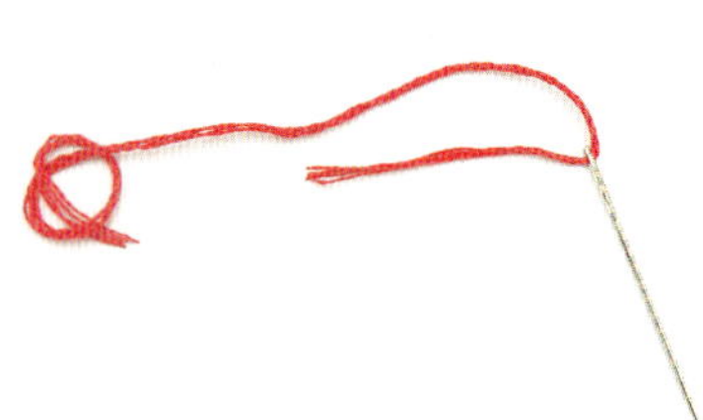

1 Make an overhand knot, which can be done with either one or several wraps of the thread tip around the rest of the thread (one wrap shown in the photograph).

2 Pull on the thread to tighten the knot. The knot usually appears some way away from the thread tip.

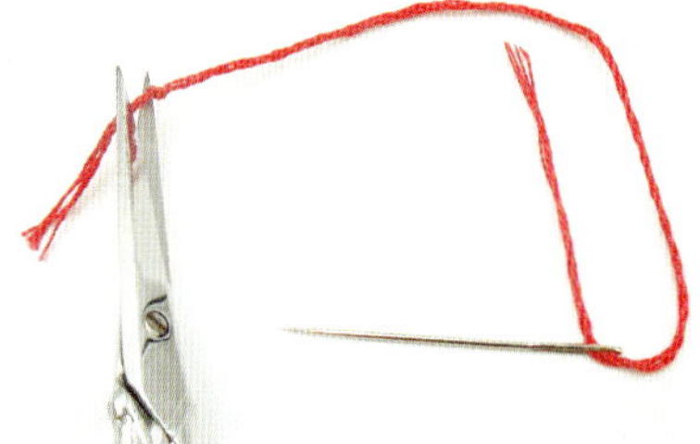

3 It's a good habit to trim away the excess thread close to the knot before you start stitching. This excess thread can bring fibres to the right side of the fabric or cause unwanted knots.

THE PROCESS OF STITCHING

Start a stitch line

Make sure the knotted tail of your thread is longer than the loose tail, then bring the needle *to the right side* of the fabric at the beginning of a stitch line (the anchoring knot tail should be on the back of the fabric).

Work the first stitch: if you have to come down next to the anchoring knot on the back, make sure you do not go through the knot. Gently move the knot to the side with your non-stitching hand, as you bring the needle through the fabric.

Ways of stitching: stabbing vs sewing

As you stitch, one movement of your needle should either bring the thread to the back side of the fabric, or to the right side. Never go down and come up in one movement!

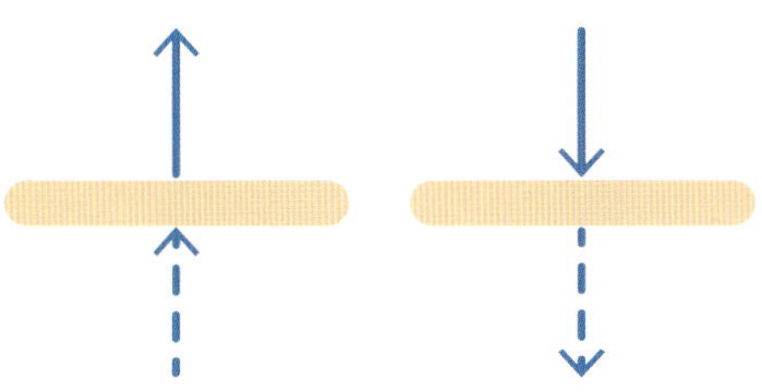

Stabbing: good for embroidery.

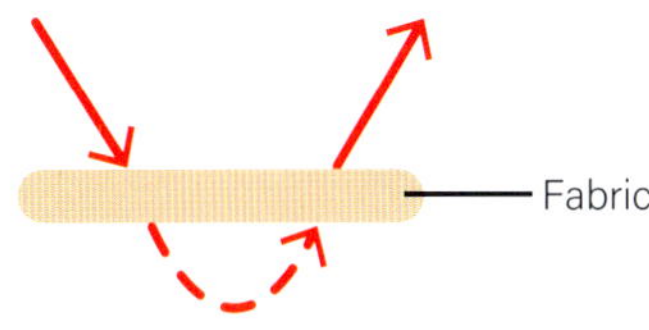

Sewing: not to be used for embroidery.

Busy place

Whenever possible, try to pass the needle downwards in places where several stitches come through the same hole in the fabric (see the photograph below and 'busy place' in the Glossary, page 26).

Stitches on the back of the fabric

These are called supporting stitches, as they hold the stitching on the right side in place. Supporting stitches should be neither too long, or too short. Too-long supporting stitches may cause contraction of the fabric, and too-short supporting stitches may accidentally unpick.

If you want to move your needle across the back of your work by more than about 1cm (½in), it is better to anchor your thread and make a fresh start.

The longer (up to 1cm/½in) and shorter (about 1mm) supporting stitches on the back of the fabric.

UNWANTED KNOTS

As you stitch, your thread may get knotted. The two issues below are the most common causes of unwanted knots in your thread. Learn how to cope with them, and your stitching will never be 'knotty' again!

Issue 1: excess twist in the thread
Thread gets more and more twisted in the process of stitching.

Solution: 'pet' the thread
To get rid of this extra twist, perform the following procedure every now and then:

1 Bring the needle to the right side and move it all the way down to the fabric, sliding the needle eye along the thread.

2 Grab the thread with your finger and thumb, close to where the thread comes out of the fabric.

3 Gently move your finger and thumb up along the thread – as if you were 'petting' the thread. Repeat this several times until the thread becomes untwisted and you feel it becoming softer.

Issue 2: loose tail of thread turns into a 'tassel'
Owing to the repeated passing through the fabric, the fibres of the loose thread tail untwist, resembling a tassel.

Solution: refresh the loose tail
As you stitch, check what the loose thread tail looks like. Spotting a tassel on its tip, trim off about 1cm (½in) of the tail to refresh it and prevent it from knotting or getting tangled with the rest of the thread.

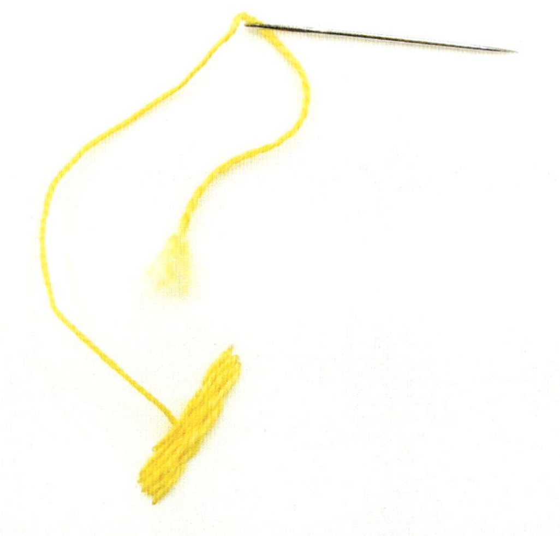

A tassel on the loose thread tail, caused by the friction against the fabric.

ENDING A STITCH

Once you have completed a stitch, bring the needle to the back of the fabric to anchor the thread tail. This can be done in a few ways; the two most common are shown in the photograph on the right.

Option 1 (shown in orange thread): take your needle under three or four stitches on the back of your work and trim off the excess thread. (It may be helpful to refer to the whipping technique, page 41, as the procedure is very similar.)

Option 2 (shown in blue thread): bring the needle underneath all of the stitches in a densely stitched area on the back of the work – if you have any close by. Repeat two or three time to anchor the thread securely. Do not worry if your needle pierces any threads on the back: doing so only provides a more secure anchor for the thread tail.

If your thread is not long enough to work the whole line or area of a stitch, anchor the thread tail on the back as described above, thread a fresh length of thread and continue stitching.

Note: think twice before deciding to preserve thread leftovers. Usually the remaining part of your thread is worn away and looks dull. Dispose of it without hesitation: the quality of your embroidery is incomparably more precious than a small piece of thread. Besides, short pieces of thread are inconvenient to stitch with.

BLOCKING YOUR FINISHED EMBROIDERY

Stitched designs will show the distinct marks of embroidery hoops on the fabric. Ironing is not the best solution, for it will make threads look dull and the stitches flat. Is it better to perform a curious procedure known as blocking or damp stretching. You will need:

- a cork pinboard (large enough for your fabric)
- push pins
- clear plastic
- a spray bottle filled with clean water.

The blocking process

1 Draw a line over the cork board, parallel to one of the sides of the board. Cover the board with a sheet of clear plastic.

2 Place your fabric onto the board, the embroidery design facing up. Pin one side of the fabric (the top of your embroidery) to the board, so that it is lined up with the straight edge. Push in the pins every 1cm (½in).

3 Pin the opposite (bottom) edge in a similar way. It is easier to start from the centre of the edge and pin the right-hand side of the fabric first, then pin to the other side, making sure the grain of the fabric is straight.

4 Pin the remaining two sides of the fabric, spray it thoroughly with water and let it dry: creases will disappear as if by magic!

READING THE EMBROIDERY INSTRUCTIONS IN THIS BOOK

This book features embroidery designs of different types. Most of the instructions are arranged to reflect the most convenient sequence of work: stitch the areas one by one, in the order shown in the instructions.

Quite a few designs include repetitive elements, to give you more practice. Some of these designs are symmetrical: work the same element over each of the parts in turn, before proceeding to the next element. Others are composed of a few types of elements, combined together to form the whole design. For these, work the type 1 elements over the whole design before proceeding to type 2, and so on.

The fabric and needles required to embroider each design are not mentioned in the instructions; instead follow the guidance outlined on pages 8 and 18.

Abbreviations

The project instructions in this book use the following abbreviations:

P5	DMC pearl cotton thread, size 5
P8	DMC pearl cotton thread, size 8
P12	DMC pearl cotton thread, size 12
P12A	Anchor pearl cotton thread, size 12
SC	DMC stranded cotton thread

Unless otherwise specified, use pearl cotton thread of any size as a single thread, for example:

P5-01 is for DMC pearl cotton, size 5 in colour no. 01 (Grey)

P8-899 is for DMC pearl cotton, size 8 in colour no. 899 (Medium Pink)

P12-3865 is for DMC pearl cotton, size 12 in colour no. 3865 (Winter White)

P12A-256 is for Anchor pearl cotton, size 12 in colour no. 256 (Olive)

The number of threads of stranded cotton needed for a particular stitch is specified by the number in brackets:

SC-165(1) is for one thread of DMC stranded cotton of colour no. 165 (Moss Green – very light)

SC-818(2) is for two threads of DMC stranded cotton of colour no. 818 (Baby Pink)

SC-3345(6) is for six threads of DMC stranded cotton of colour no. 3345 (Hunter Green – dark)

Couching SC-3326(6;2) means couching technique, with six laid threads of stranded cotton and two tying threads of stranded cotton, both in colour no. 3326 (Rose – light)

SAMPLE INSTRUCTIONS

TEXT IN THE INSTRUCTIONS	WHAT YOU WILL NEED TO DO
Foliage **1** Stem stitch P8-320	**Step 1** Using size 8 DMC pearl cotton thread of colour number 320 (Medium Pistachio Green), work stem stitch along the line marked in number 1.
2 Fly stitch leaf P12-503	**Step 2** Work the smaller leaf in fly stitch leaf technique, using size 12 DMC pearl cotton thread of colour number 503 (Medium Blue Green).
3 Fly stitch leaf P8-320	**Step 3** Work the bigger leaf in fly stitch leaf technique, using size 8 DMC pearl cotton thread of colour number 320 (Medium Pistachio Green).
4 Fly stitch liana P8-320 and P5-01	**Step 4** Using the fly stitch liana technique, work the upwards-facing triangles, using size 8 DMC pearl cotton thread of colour number 320 (Medium Pistachio Green). Change to size 5 DMC pearl cotton thread of colour number 01 (Grey) and work triangles facing downwards.

Glossary

The description of stitches in the embroidery instructions mention some terms which may be new to you.

ANCHORING VS LOOSE THREAD TAILS As embroidery is usually worked in single thread, the longer thread tail with the knotted tip is called anchoring (since it helps to attach a length of thread to the fabric), and the shorter one is called loose, because... it is loose!

BUSY PLACE A spot where two or more stitches meet: a hole in the fabric through which the needle has already passed several times. If possible, always bring the needle down through a busy place – it will make your stitching easier and more precise.

HOLE IN FABRIC The space between threads, woven into fabric. If you are advised to stitch through the same hole in the fabric, it simply means you are to go repeatedly through exactly the same place.

INDIVIDUAL STITCH One stitch which, when worked repeatedly, forms a stitch line.

KEY MOVE The movement which should be worked repeatedly to form a stitch. The term highlights the principal movement needed to build up a stitch.

RIVER BANK RULE Remember what we were taught at school: stand on a bridge over a river, with your face turned in the direction the water is flowing. The side of the river on your left hand is the left river bank, and the side on your right hand is the right bank. The same can be applied to a stitch line, referring to the direction of stitching. In the photograph below left, the area marked hatched is the right side of the stich line. Remember this rule to determine sides: some stitches get the proper look only if thread is placed over a particular side.

The River Bank Rule.

A stitch line.

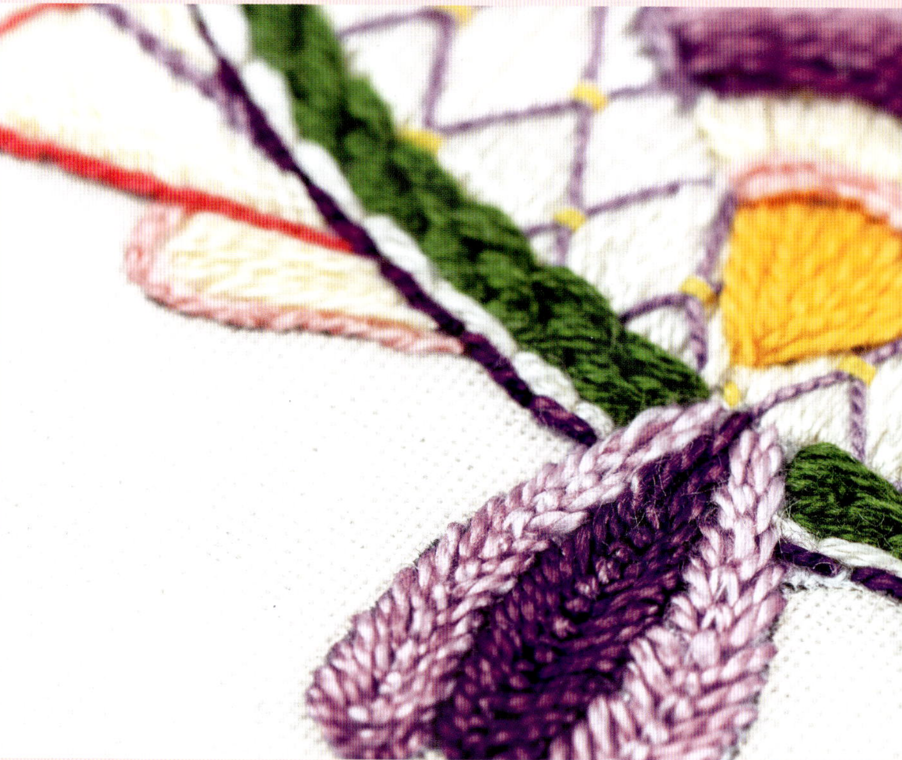

STITCH LINE A number of stitches of the same kind, worked along a straight, curved or angled line (see photograph, bottom right).

STITCHING ZONE An area of an embroidery design to be covered with a particular type of stitch.

SUPPORTING STITCH A stitch that goes on the back of the fabric and joins neighbouring stitches on the right side.

TEST STITCHING Working a stitch on a spare piece of fabric, either as a learning exercise, or for testing the look of a stitch worked in a particular thread. Also known as doodle stitching. You may want to keep a piece of fabric (a doodle cloth) as a reminder of your stitching experiments, or even turn your doodle stitching into a piece of artwork! Remember to do some test stitching before you start to embroider a design, to practise the stitches.

TO COME UP Bring the needle to the right side of the fabric.

TO GO DOWN Bring the needle to the back side of the fabric (also known as 'go to the back').

TO WORK IN SEVERAL JOURNEYS To complete a stitch in several passes, working them from left to right and then the opposite direction.

TYING STITCHES Very short straight stitches (or even small loops, formed by coming through the same hole in the fabric), worked around some threads to anchor them to the fabric. Also known as couching stitches.

TYING THREAD A length of finer thread used to anchor a heavier thread to the fabric.

Techniques

and projects

Techniques

STRAIGHT STITCH

Straight stitch is an icon of simplicity. Still, it provides awesome opportunities – have a look for yourself!

1 The needle just comes up and goes down.

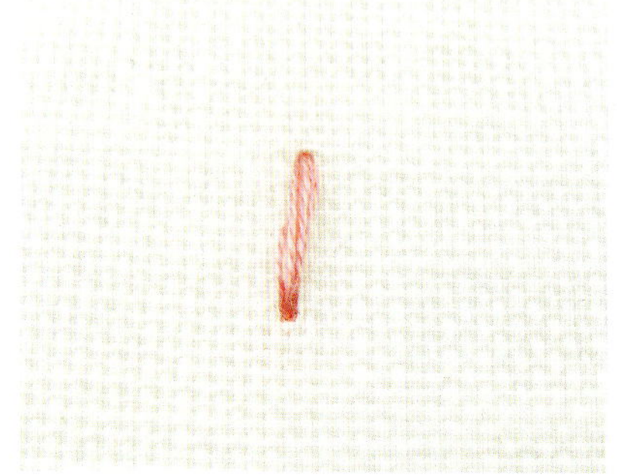

2 The length of the finished stitch may vary from 3–10mm (⅛–½in).

ARROWHEAD STITCH

Work three straight stitches, which fan out from the same spot in the fabric.

1 Work a vertical straight stitch.

2 Add one straight stitch on the left and one straight stitch on the right. Now all the three stitches are fanning out of the same spot. Yet, the side stitches are worked *towards* that spot and not *out of* it, following the 'busy place' rule (see page 21).

Arrowhead variations can be created by simply extending the length of the central stitch.

SHIFT STITCH

Either work shift stitch in one colour, or use a different thread for the tying stitch, as shown below.

1 Work three straight stitches with small gaps between them.

2 Come up through one gap.

3 Take your needle around the three stitches, and go down, as shown.

4 This gives you a tying stitch.

5 Tighten the tying stitch to finish.

One- and two-coloured variations of shift stitch.

RUNNING STITCH

Running stitch is a distinct representative of the so-called line stitches, as it forms a line. The magic of line stitches is that they may be used for filling also: just work them in parallel lines!

1 Repeatedly work straight stitches to form a line.

Place rows side by side to create a filling.

WHIPPED RUNNING STITCH

To whip a stitch means to go round it with another thread. Whipping is an easy way to alter the look of a stitch. Use either toning or contrasting thread for whipping.

1 Work a line of running stitches. Come up at the one end of the stitch line.

2 Go *under* every single stitch in turn. Go down at the other end of the stitch line.

STEM STITCH VS OUTLINE STITCH

How do we know which of the river banks is the left one? Surely, by referring to the direction of a river's flow. Now think of a stitch line as a river. Judging on which direction the stitch goes, see its right and left sides.

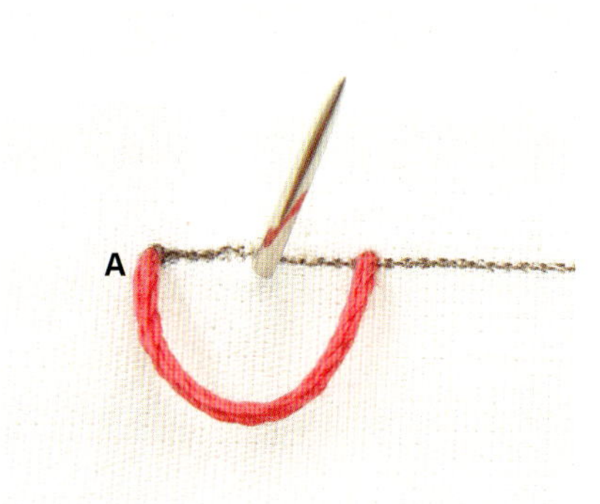

1 Come up at A. Work a loose straight stitch, placing it on the right. Come up for the next stitch.

2 Go down to finish the second stitch. The first stitch is shown untightened for clarity.

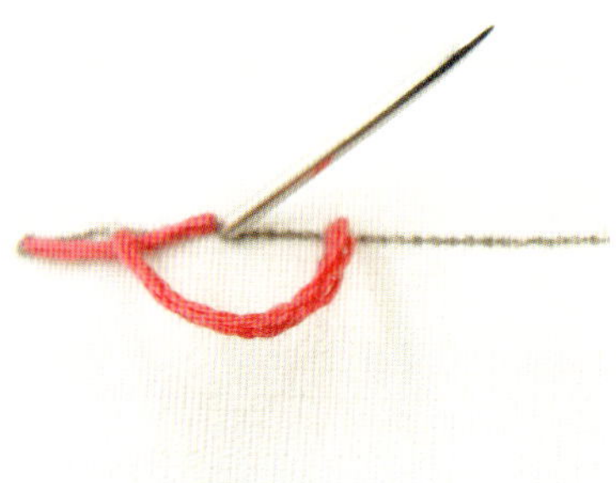

3 Come up for the third stitch. The second stitch is shown untightened for clarity.

4 Go down at the end of the stitch line.

Stem stitch filling

I love this way of imitating silk shading as it is quicker and easier to do.

Work parallel rows of stem stitch, placing them side by side. Remember the River Bank Rule (see page 26) to get a consistent look for the filling. The photograph above shows threads of contrasting colours for you to see the rows; you can use the same thread.

Outline stitch

Outline stitch is a variation of stem stitch. Just place the loop over the other side (over the 'left bank,' as shown in pale pink in the photograph), as you work the stitch. It is unbelievable, but the stitch line will look finer and less twisted. That is because of the twist in threads: stem stitch emphasizes it and outline stitch eliminates it.

Gum Tree Leaves

An iconic symbol of Australia, gum trees or eucalyptus are amazing in so many ways! Some species have capsules that are sealed with resin which melts by the heat of a fire, thus releasing the seeds. Their leathery leaves can survive drought, their roots allow regrowth after being burnt, and their aromatic oil is widely used in medicine and cosmetics.

This design features natural gum tree leaves, which I gathered on the banks of the Yarra river in Melbourne and arranged as a herbarium, with some eucalyptus flowers added here and there. The original embroidery is worked in stranded cotton threads, but you can certainly replace them with pearl cotton threads of size 8 or 12.

Also remember to do some doodle-stitching to learn embroidery techniques before you start working on the actual design.

SIZE

Approximately 12 x 11.5cm (4¾ x 4½in)

THREADS

DMC stranded cotton thread (SC):

335 Rose
165 Moss Green – very light
471 Avocado Green – very light
470 Avocado Green – light
3345 Hunter Green – dark

PATTERN NOTES

This design features a number of arrowheads, evenly placed along the design line. The easiest way to do this is to stitch them in two journeys. On the first journey, work the central stitches of each of the clusters. On the return journey, add two side stitches (to the right and to the left of the central stitch).

The instructions use some abbreviations of thread names, see page 24.

STITCHES USED

- Straight stitch, see page 30
- Arrowhead stitch, see page 30
- Shift stitch, see page 31
- Running stitch (line and filling), see page 32
- Stem stitch (line and filling), see page 33

INSTRUCTIONS

This design is composed using elements of four different types. First embroider elements of type 1 over the whole design, then proceed to type 2 and so on.

1 Eucalypt blossom

1a Flowers in full bloom: straight stitch SC-335(2). First work straight stitches on the sides; then add one more stitch in the centre. Finally, fill in the remaining space, so the stitches evenly radiate from the centre.

1b Flower buds: arrowhead stitch SC-335(2).

1c Flower cups: arrowhead SC-3345(2).

1d Twigs: stem stitch SC-3345(2).

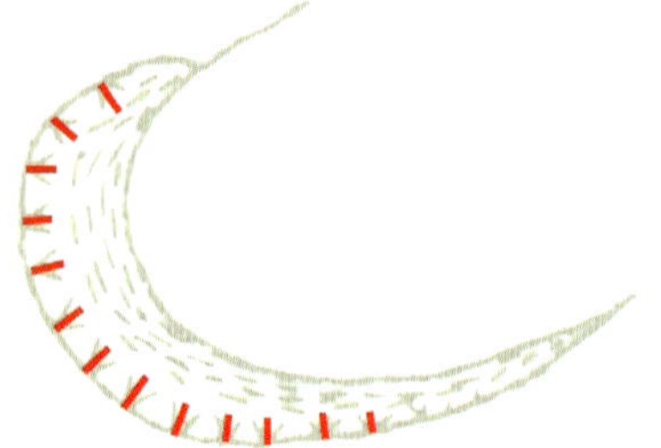

First journey

2 Openwork leaves

Outline: stem stitch in SC-3345(2) or SC-471(2).

Filling: running stitch (as a line or filling) in either SC-3345(1 or 2) or SC-471(1 or 2); arrowhead in either SC-3345(2) or SC-471(2). To place evenly spaced arrowheads, work central stitches for each arrowhead first. After that it is easy to add stitches to the right and to the left of the central stitch.

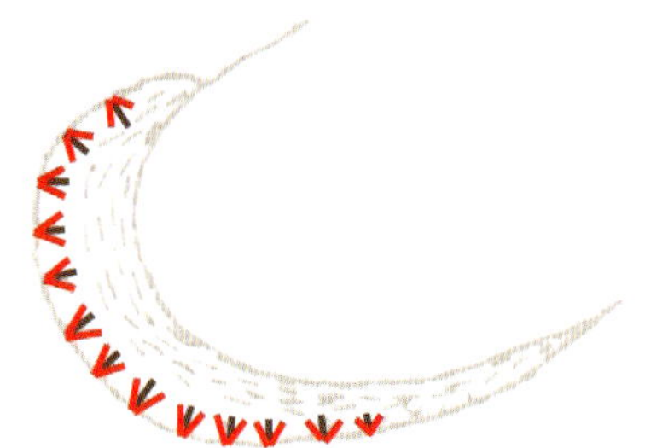

Second journey

3 Solid leaves

Stem stitch filling: use either SC-3345(2) or SC-470(2).

4 Gum tree pollen (the enlarged imitation of it)

Shift stitch SC-165(1).

4
1d
3
2
1c
1b
2
1b
1
1d
1c
1c
3
1a

Techniques

LAZY DAISY STITCH VS LONG-TAILED DAISY

Lazy daisy stitch is formed by a loop being anchored to fabric by a tiny straight stitch, known as tying stitch. Lengthen the tying stitch, and you will make a long-tailed daisy.

1 Make a loop: come up and go down through the same or neighbouring spots.

2 The finished loop.

3 Work a tying stitch: come up inside the loop.

4 Go down outside the loop.

Variations: long-tailed lazy daisy (top) and lazy daisy (bottom; also known as daisy stitch).

CHAIN STITCH VS REVERSE CHAIN

Chain stitch forms a line. One end of the line is lazy daisy (red in the photograph) and the other end is a loop (pale pink in the photograph on the right). Chain stitch can be worked from either end, developing the same look. The easier way is to start with lazy daisy stitch, as below. This method is called reverse chain, and you will find the regular way of working chain stitch in Going further (page 118).

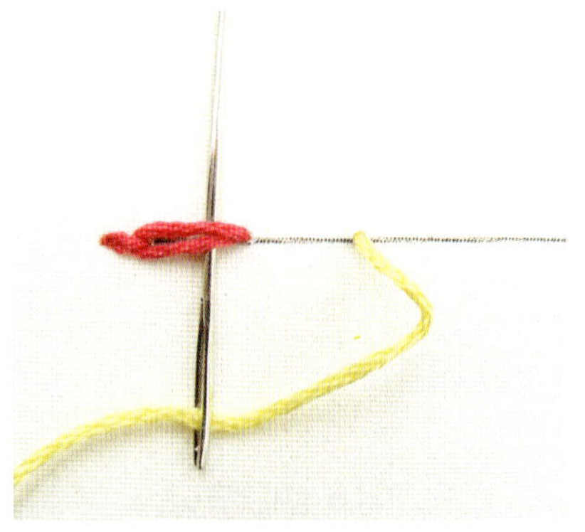

1 Work a lazy daisy stitch (red); and come up for the next stitch (yellow). Bring the needle underneath the threads of the lazy daisy stitch.

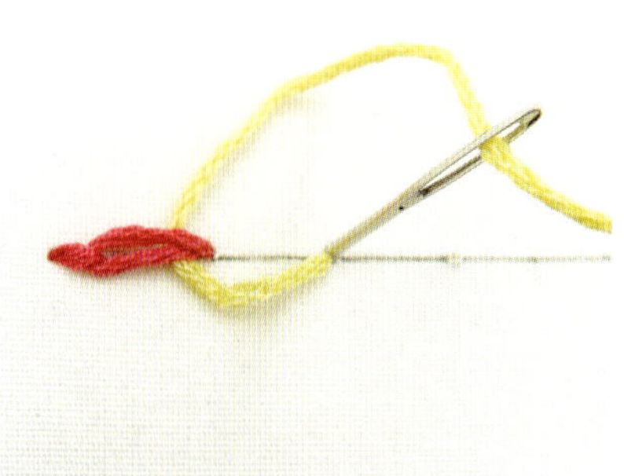

2 Go down to make a loop. Making loops is the Key Move for this stitch.

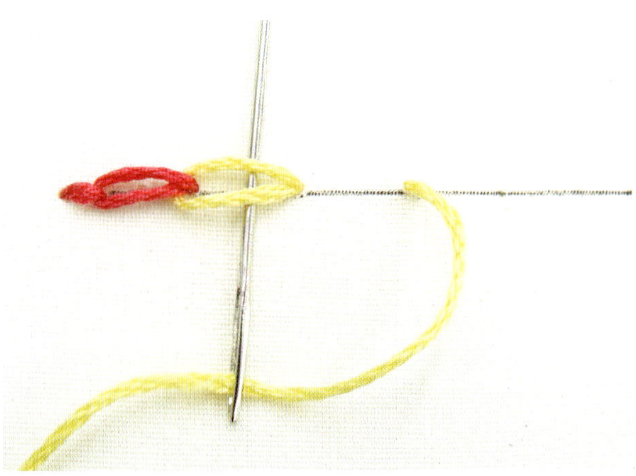

3 Keep making loops along the stitch line. Work as many loops as you need for your stitch line.

4 The two-coloured chain stitch is shown for clarity with enlarged loops. The chain stitch shown in red has loops of normal size.

TULIP STITCH

Work this stitch in one or two colours. Contrasting thread is used below for clarity.

1 Work a daisy stitch, then add a straight stitch, bringing the needle underneath the tying stitch.

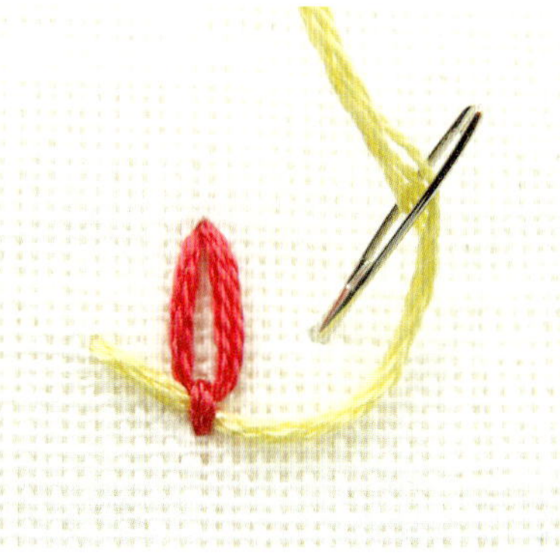

2 Bring the needle to the back of the fabric.

3 The finished tulip stitch.

OX HEAD STITCH

This is a very old stitch with a funny name. Can you spot the head of an ox in the shape?

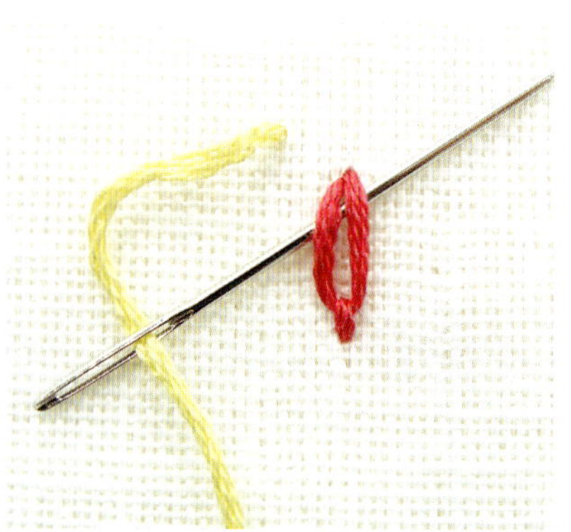

1 Work a daisy stitch, then add a straight stitch from one side of the daisy to the other, bringing the needle underneath the top of the loop.

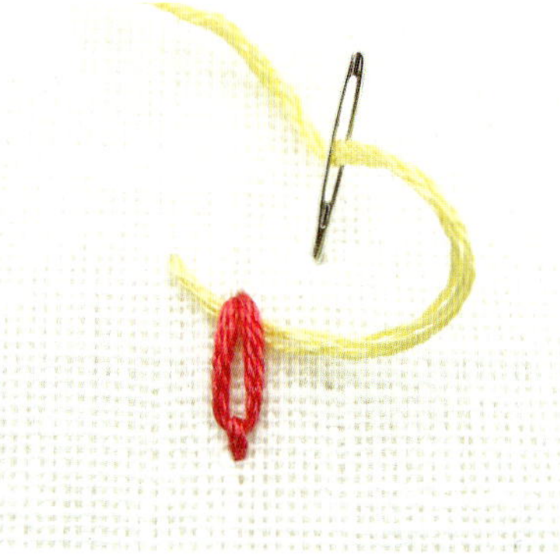

2 Go down opposite the start of the straight stitch.

3 The finished ox head. Two colours are shown for clarity.

WHIPPED CHAIN – THREE WAYS

You can use the same colour or a contrasting thread for whipping. Come up at the beginning of the stitch line, whip the thread around the stitches, following one of the three patterns shown below. Go down at the end.

Whipped chain

1 Bring the needle underneath both halves of a loop.

2 Continue whipping in the same way to the end of the stitch line, and bring the needle to the back of the fabric.

Whipped chain – one side

Whip one side of each loop of the chain stitch, bringing the needle from the outer side towards the centre of a loop.

Whipped chain – each side

Come up at A and follow the instructions for whipping one side of chain; go down at B. Come up at C to whip the other side. Note the direction of whipping (from the centre of a loop towards the outer side), to get a nice pattern as shown in the photograph.

LATTICE

This stitch has three stages: the bottom layer, top layer and tying stitches. Decide on the shape of the cells before you start stitching – they can be square or diamond shaped.

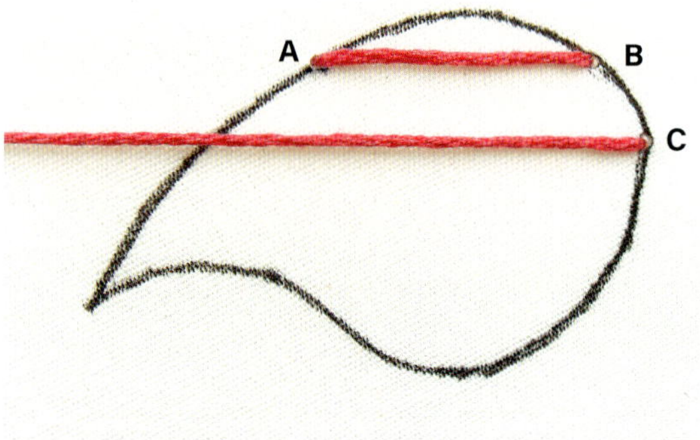

1 Start with the bottom layer: make a long straight stitch. You will want to add more stitches evenly spaced and parallel to each other below this stitch. To work out a neat placement for the end of a stitch, lay the thread across the fabric to check the lines look parallel before you complete the stitch.

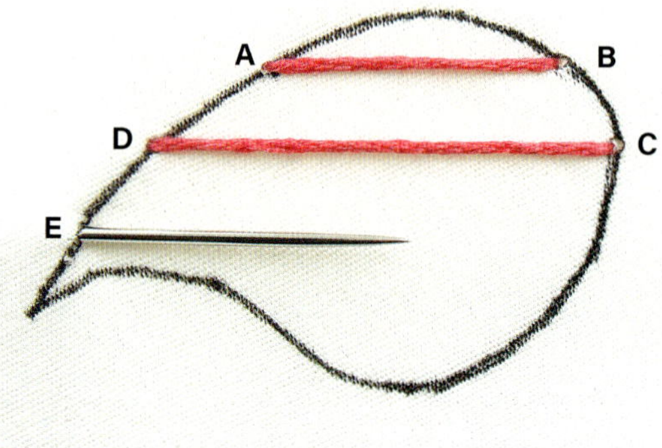

2 Find the starting point for the next stitch: bring the needle halfway through the fabric, place it against the fabric, and see whether you are happy with the spacing before completing the stitch.

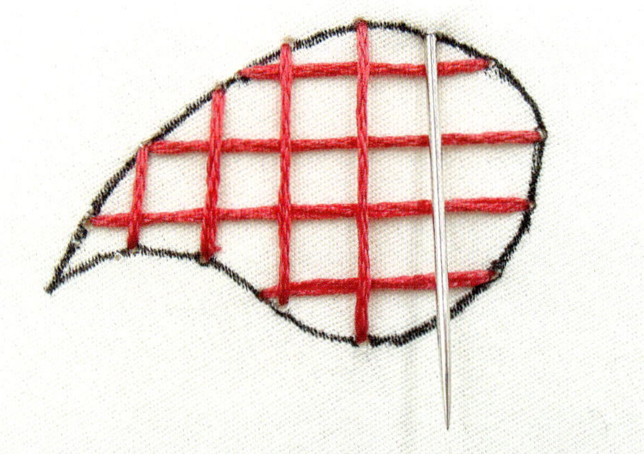

3 Add the top layer. Add vertical stitches over the top of the horizontal ones. Use the above tips to figure out where to start and finish each stitch.

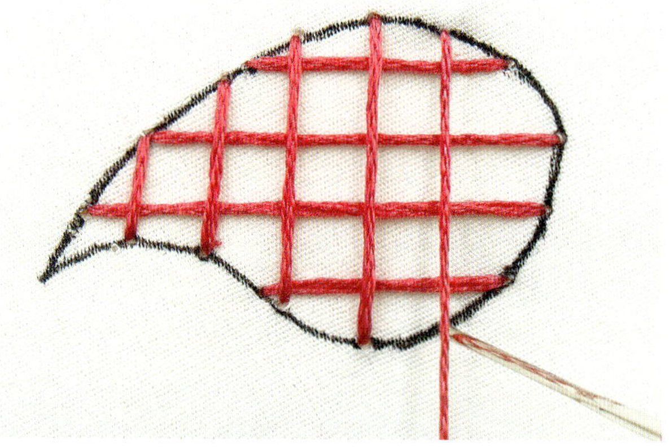

4 Continue adding vertical lines to create a grid shape. In the photograph, stitches on the top layer go at right angles to stitches on the bottom layer, which makes square cells. Place them at a different angle to make diamond-shaped cells.

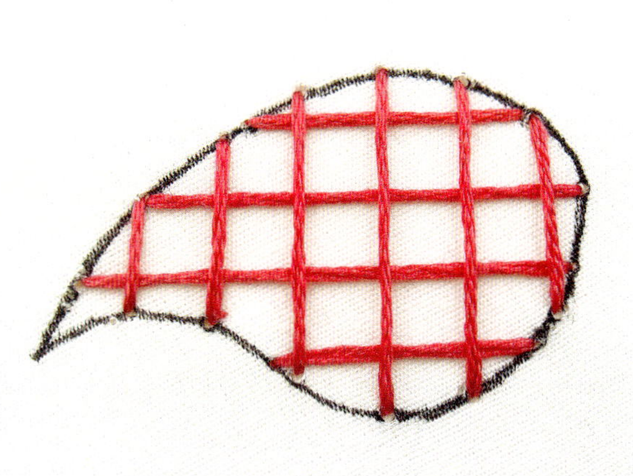

5 The grid is complete and ready to add the tying stitches in the next step.

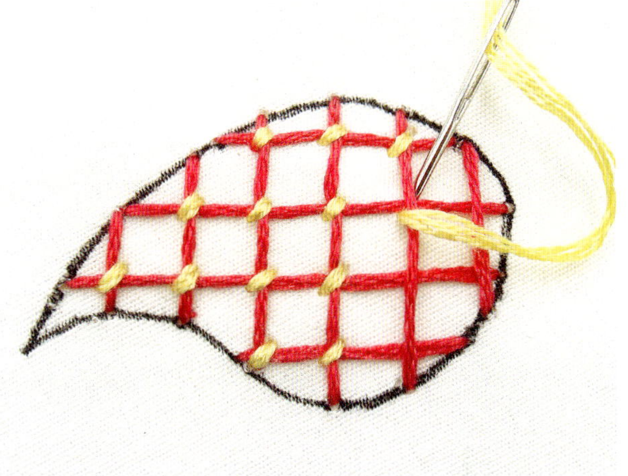

6 Use finer thread of a contrasting colour. Work one small diagonal tying stitch at each intersection. It is a good habit to couch all the intersections along one line (any line, either vertical or horizontal) before you move to the next line to prevent missing an intersection.

7 Optional: if preferred, you could work two tying stitches at each intersection.

Two ways of working tying stitches. Work tying stitches in finer thread even for doodle-stitching. The cross stitch at the intersection looks untidy because of the thickness of the tying thread, used here for clarity.

Morning Glory

Symmetrical designs are especially good for beginners, allowing you to practise stitches while working similar areas. Do not be confused if your stitching on the right is not the mirror image of that on the left: that is normal for hand embroidery. On the contrary, connoisseur collectors of hand embroidery samples check whether those samples have slight imperfections to know they were really stitched by hand. Besides, have ever you seen any ideal symmetry in nature?!

The charming flowers of morning glory come in a vast variety of colours. Would you like to try a different colour scheme for your stitching?

SIZE

Approximately 14 x 11cm (5½ x 4¼in)

MATERIALS

DMC pearl cotton thread, size 8 (P8):

899 Rose – medium

DMC stranded cotton thread (SC):

335 Rose
818 Baby Pink
3326 Rose – light
165 Moss Green – very light
471 Avocado Green – very light
470 Avocado Green –light
3345 Hunter Green – dark
726 Topaz – light

PATTERN NOTES

Though the design is symmetrical, its right- and left-hand halves are stitched with few alterations, mostly slight variations in thread colour. Therefore, you have a choice to either repeat it as it is, or to choose your favourite side and duplicate it for the other half of the design.

The instructions use some abbreviations of thread names, see page 24.

STITCHES USED

- Lazy daisy, see page 38
- Reverse chain stitch (line and filling), see page 39
- Tulip stitch, see page 40
- Ox head stitch, see page 40
- Whipped chain stitch, see page 41
- Lattice, see page 42
- Straight stitch, see page 30
- Shift stitch, see page 31
- Running stitch filling, see page 32
- Stem stitch (line and filling), see page 33

INSTRUCTIONS

Numbers 1–13b indicate the sequence of stitching. The instructions below refer to the left-hand side embroidery, unless otherwise stated.

1 Chain stitch, one side whipped SC-335(3;4).
Optional: stem stitch along the inner side of the chain and very close to it SC-818(2).

2 Lattice P8-899; tying stitches in SC-818(2).

3a Tulip stitch SC-818(2).

3b Ox head stitch SC-818(2).

4 Stem stitch filling P8-899. **On the right:** chain stitch filling P8-899.

5 Straight stitches, radiating from the flower centre SC-726(1).

6 Running stitch filling (three rows) SC-3326(1). I would rather *not* mark the lines for running stitch, since they would not be covered with the actual stitching. Instead, make holes in the fabric with a large needle to mark the central of the three lines. Follow these marks to work the first running stitch, and then add one more stitch line on each side.

7 Chain stitch: one line in SC-3345(2); two lines in SC-471(2). **On the right:** same stitch, one line in SC-470(2); two lines in SC-165(2) and one line in SC-726(2).

8 Chain stitch, one line in each of the following: SC-726(2); SC-165(2); SC-471(2). **On the right:** same stitch, one line each in SC-726(2); SC-165(2); and SC-3345(2).

9 Stem stitch filling SC-471(2). **On the right:** same technique SC-3345(2).

10 Lazy daisy stitch SC-471(2). **On the right:** same technique SC-3345(2).

11 Stem stitch SC-471(2). **On the right:** same technique SC-3345(2).

12 Chain stitch: one line in SC-726(2); three lines in SC-818(2). To outline: one line of chain stitch SC-3345(2). **On the right:** one line in SC-726(2); two lines in SC-165(2) plus one line in SC-471(2). To outline: one line of chain stitch SC-471(2).

13a Shift stitch SC-726(1). **On the right:** same technique SC-470(1).

13b Shift stitch SC-818(1). **On the right:** same technique SC-165(1).

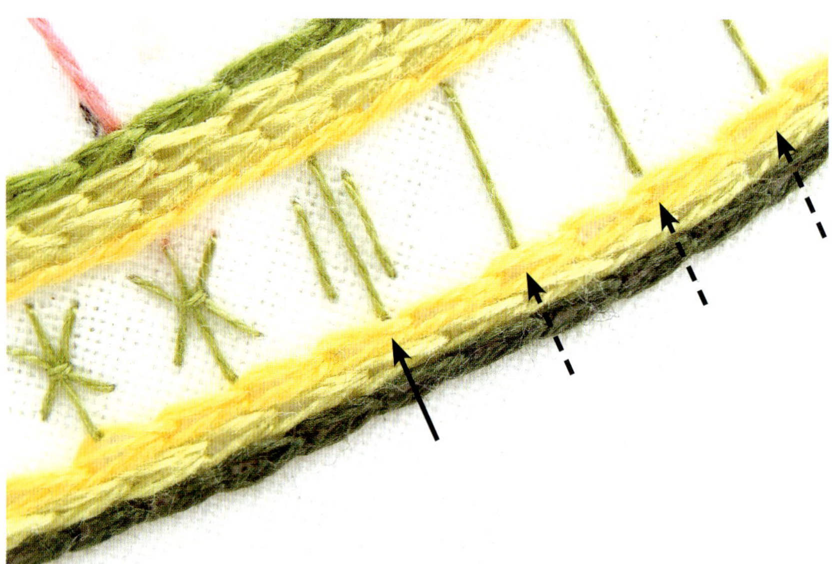

Note for zone 13a: to evenly space the shift stitches, work them in two journeys. First, work all seven central stitches (see the dashed arrows shown to the left). On the return journey, complete each of the shift stitches in turn. Work in a similar way for zone 13b.

1
2
3a
3b
4
5
6
7
8
9
10
11
12
13a
13b

Techniques

FLY STITCH – SINGLE VS STACKED

Fly stitch is actually a lazy daisy with an open (unlocked) loop. This stitch can be worked as a single stitch, or stacked (that is, several fly stitches being worked closely together).

Fly stitch – single

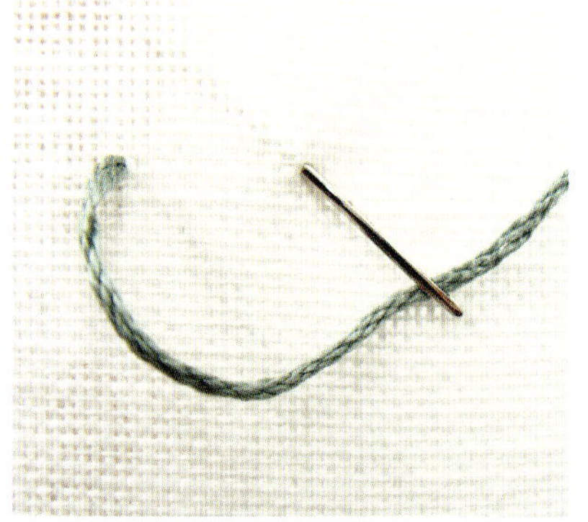

1 Work a loose straight stitch.

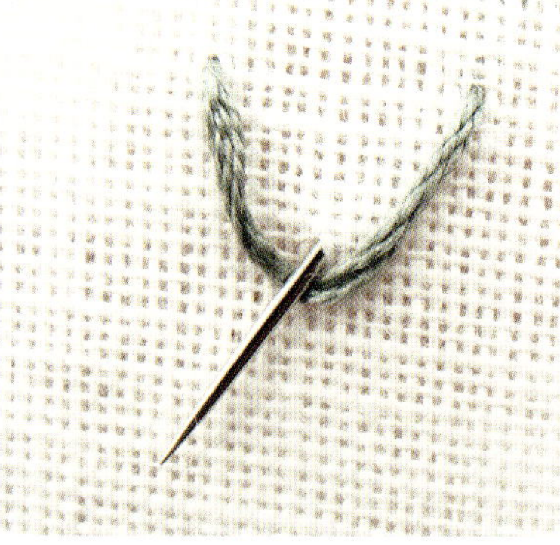

2 Come up inside the unlocked loop.

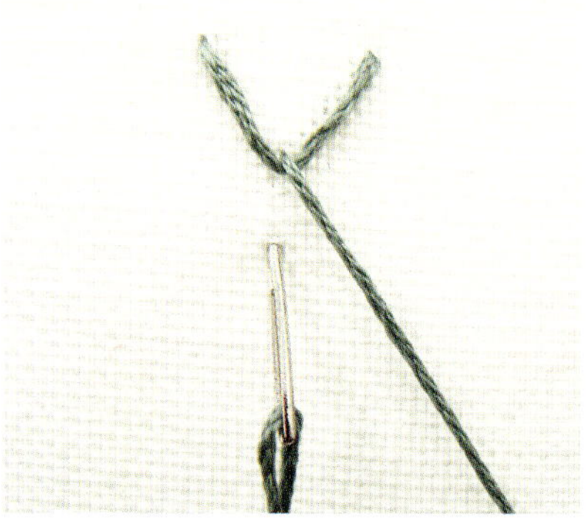

3 Go down outside the loop, thus making a tying stitch.

Finished fly stitches, with tying stitches of varying length.

Fly stitch – stacked

Work the first fly stitch (shown in black) with a very short tying stitch. Add the second and the third fly stitches (shown in red), placing them close to the first one and working them all with short tying stitches. Add as many stitches as you like, placing each next to the previous stitch.

Fly stitch – liana

Some embroidery stitches are named after the botanical terms for parts of plants (for example, stem stitch). Here is a nice technique to work some popular elements of crewel designs: lianas (woody vines), curved branches or trunks. The photograph on the right shows the liana unfinished: that is to highlight the two elements of the technique, which are to be repeatedly worked along the liana.

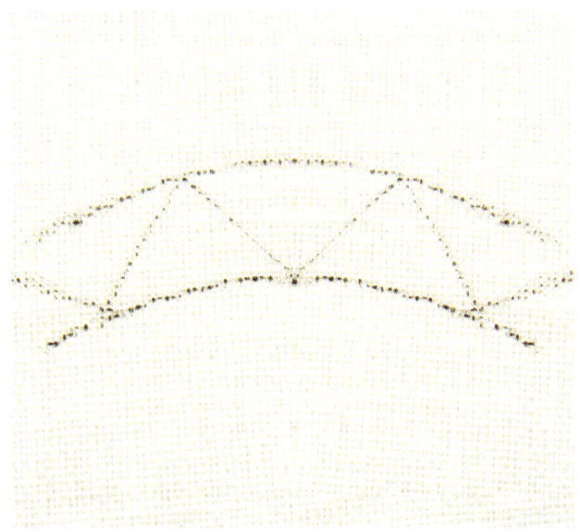

1 Divide the liana into triangles. Decide on two thread colours.

2 Fill in each triangle with stacked fly stitch, starting from the longest fly, in this case at the bottom.

3 Fill the triangles on the other side with stacked fly stitch in the same way as before, using the other thread colour.

4 Optional: work a tiny straight stitch to fill the gap in the middle.

TIP

I prefer to work all the triangles along one side before working the other side of the liana.

Fly stitch – leaf

With small alterations, stacked fly stitch can be used to create a leaf shape.

1 Work a straight stitch, which will be the tip of a leaf. Add a loop of fly stitch around it.

2 Come up inside the loop.

3 Work a very small tying stitch to hold the loop in place. Proceed in the same way, repeatedly working fly stitches close to each other, and following the leaf shape.

4 Optional: make the very last tying stitch longer to resemble the stalk of the leaf.

5 For a dentate leaf margin, lengthen some of the fly stitches.

GRANITOS

The etymology of the stitch name is fun – the Spanish word 'granito' means 'a small grain'. Consequently, granitos is plural. Do not be surprised, therefore, to see the stitch mentioned either way – it is still the same stitch. Do not change thread colour as you progress – it is worked in two colours below for clarity.

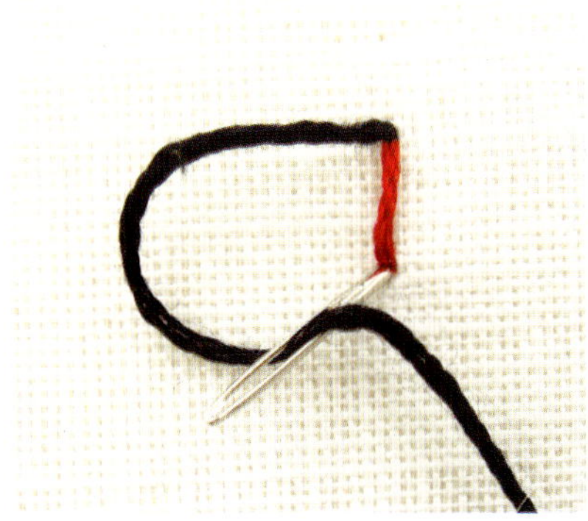

1 Work a straight stitch (shown here in red), and then add another straight stitch to the left, coming up and down through the same holes, as for the red stitch.

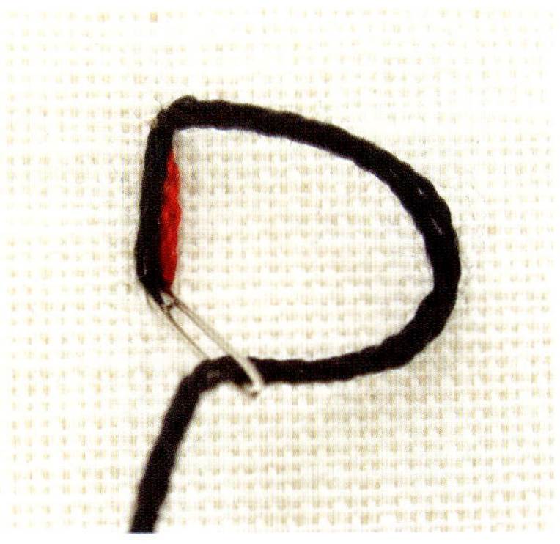

2 Add one more stitch to the right of it, coming through the *same* holes in the fabric.

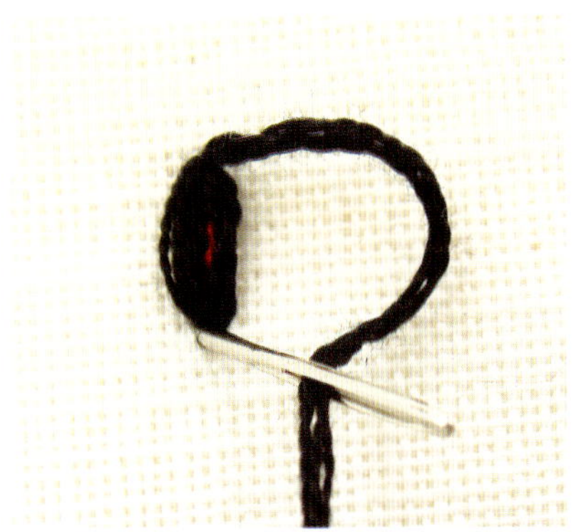

3 Add one more pair of stitches, further still to the right and to the left.

4 Add as many pairs of stitches as you like.

BLANKET VS BUTTONHOLE STITCH

Blanket stitch and buttonhole stitch are similar-looking; they differ only in the spacing of individual stitches. Work each stitch perpendicular to the stitch line, as shown below.

Blanket stitch

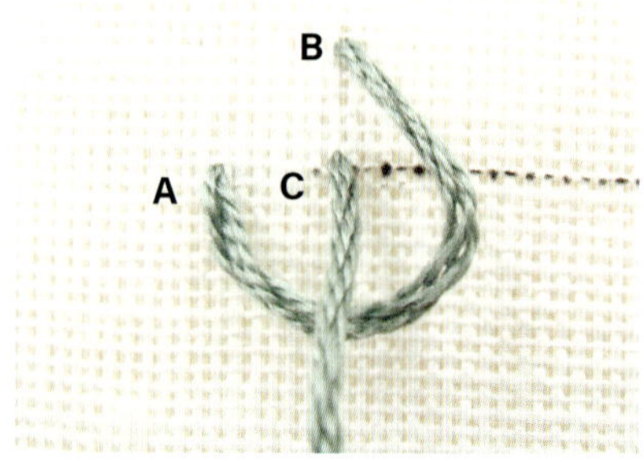

1 Come up at A, go down at B. Come up at C.

2 Tighten up the loop.

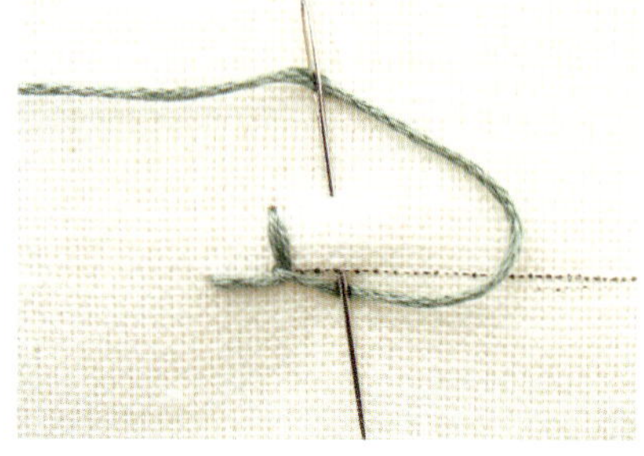

3 Work the second blanket stitch. This is the Key Move. Repeat it to the end of the stitch line.

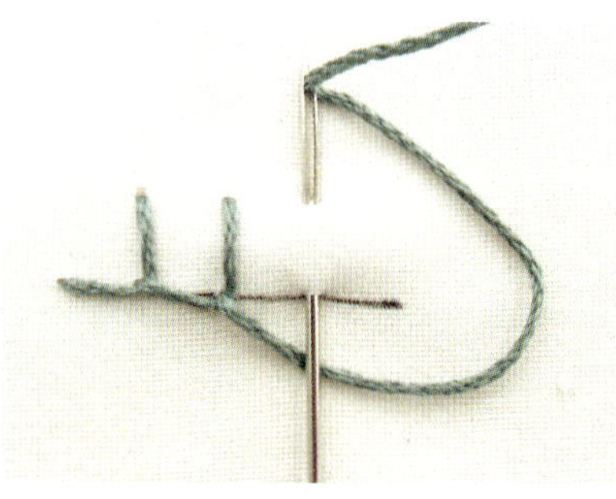

4 Repeat the Key Move to the end of the stitch line.

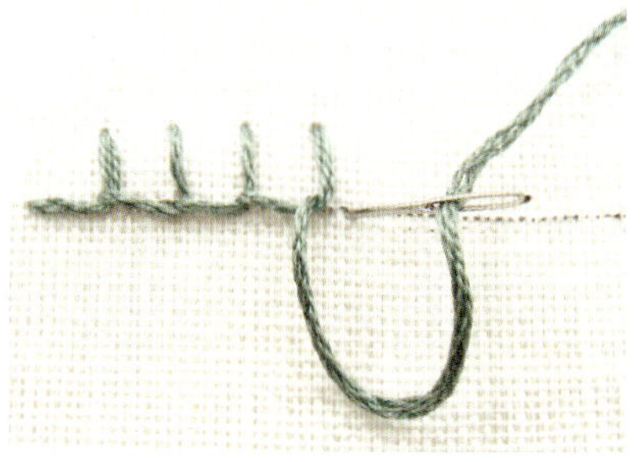

5 Go down at the end to form a tying stitch.

> **TIP**
>
> The Key Move is shown in a sewing method, but you should work the stitch in two passes, following the stabbing method (see page 21).

Buttonhole stitch

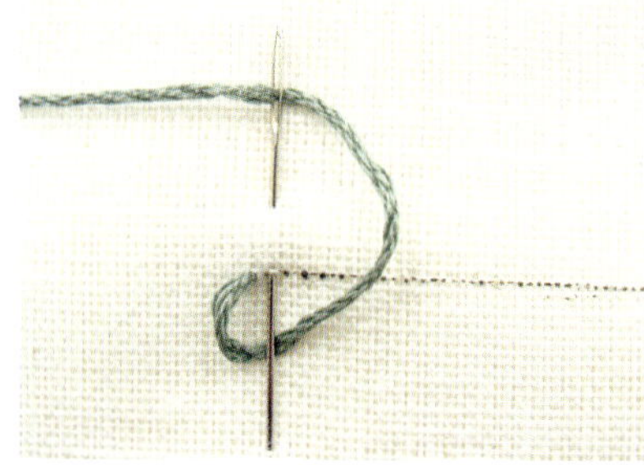

1 For buttonhole stitch, work the same Key Move...

2 ...but do not leave any space between individual stitches.

3 To finish, work a tying stitch as shown above. See how the 'height' of stitches may vary: use it to your benefit.

BUTTONHOLED CHAIN STITCH

This stitch looks equally as lovely when worked in one or two colours. Scallops are formed using detached buttonhole stitches (that is, they are detached from the fabric).

1 Work a line of chain stitch. Key Move: work a buttonhole stitch, as shown above. Do not forget that the stitch is a detached buttonhole, so do not come through the fabric. Tighten the stitch and work another stitch in the same way. Repeat until this section of thread is covered with stitching.

2 Take the needle to the back, ready to move to the next loop.

3 Continue in the same way, working to cover each loop with buttonhole stitches.

TIP

To make scallops overlap, come up through the previous loop when starting a new loop.

Crewel Poppy

A poppy is often associated with the fiery red of its tender petals, yet the variety of colours nowadays amazing! Would you like to turn the design into an alpine poppy by applying shades of yellow instead of red?

Learn the effective technique of working a leaf in fly stitch – and how to make that leaf jagged. Isn't it amazing, how professional and complex the buttonholed chain stitch looks? Perhaps you would like to apply the technique used for working poppy seedheads for your other projects.

SIZE

10 x 15cm (4 x 6in)

THREADS

DMC pearl cotton thread, size 5 (P5):

01 Grey

DMC pearl cotton thread, size 8 (P8):

817 Coral Red

320 Pistachio Green – medium

DMC pearl cotton thread, size 12 (P12):

503 Blue Green – medium

666 Christmas Red

DMC stranded cotton thread (SC):

310 Black

PATTERN NOTES

I've used a rectangular hoop, but this is optional and you can work in a round hoop just as well. You may also like to play around with the number and placement of poppy seedheads, as well as the abstract greenery.

The instructions use some abbreviations of thread names, see page 24.

STITCHES USED

- Fly stitch, see page 48
- Fly stitch – stacked, see page 48
- Fly stitch liana, see page 49
- Fly stitch leaf, see page 50
- Granitos, see page 51
- Buttonhole stitch, see page 52
- Buttonholed chain stitch, see page 53
- Blanket stitch (arranged in semi-circle), see page 56
- Straight stitch, see page 30
- Running stitch, see page 32
- Stem stitch, see page 33
- Long-tailed daisy stitch, see page 38
- Chain stitch, see page 39
- Lattice, see page 42

INSTRUCTIONS

Flower

1 Blanket stitch P8-320, arranged in a semi-circle (to do this, work blanket stitches radiating from the centre of that circle, starting them all from the same hole in the fabric, as shown below). Straight stitches inside the gaps P5-01.

2 Lattice P8-817, tying stitches P12-666. Fill in the cells with long-tailed daisy stitches P12-666 (see Tip opposite).

3 Granitos SC-310(3). Straight stitches radiating from the centre SC-310(3).

4 Buttonholed chain stitch: P5-01 for the chain, and P8-817 for detached buttonhole stitches.

5 Buttonhole stitch P8-817.
Optional: work guiding stitches first. That is, work seven or eight straight stitches in P12-666, fanning them out a little. These stitches will help you see the proper inclination of buttonhole stitches. The guiding stitches are not meant to be covered with buttonhole. Instead, they add a fresh shade to the petal.

6 Blanket stitch P12-666. Place the stitches fanning out, following the shape of the petals.

7 Straight stitches of varying length P12-666 inside each gap.

TIP

Both buttonhole and blanket stitch can be arranged in a semi-circle (known as buttonhole scallop, disregarding the actual spacing in stitches).

Bring the needle down through the same hole in the fabric, to make individual stitches meet in the centre of a semi-circle.

You may find it more convenient to start a scallop with a straight stitch, as shown in red thread in the photograph on the right.

TIP

An easy way to make the long-tailed daisies the same size is to start from the centre of a cell and work a tying stitch for each daisy (the top row in the photograph on the right). Repeat across the lattice and then attach a tiny loop (the bottom row in the photograph on the right).

Foliage

1 Stem stitch P8-320.

2 Fly stitch leaf P12-503.

3 Fly stitch leaf P8-320.

4 Fly stitch liana P8-320 and P5-01.

5 Fly stitch liana P12-503 and P5-01.

6 Poppy seedheads are worked from A–C (see below).

7 Stacked fly stitch P8-320 (or P12-503).

8 Abstract greenery: running stitch P8-320 (or P12-503).

9 Frame: one long straight stitch per each of the four sides. One thread of each of the following: SC-310(1), P8-320 and P12-503. Note that the frame is not marked on the template; it is for you to arrange to your liking, or leave off altogether if you prefer.

Poppy seedheads

A Top part: granitos P5-01.
Middle part: straight stitches P5-01.
Tiny bottom part: a small daisy stitch P5-01.

B Top part: fanning out straight stitches P12-666.

C Middle part: straight stitches P8-320 (or P12-503).
Tiny bottom part: a small daisy stitch P8-320 (or P12-503).

1
2
3
4
5
6
7
8
9

Techniques

BACKSTITCH, SEEDING STITCH AND SPLIT BACKSTITCH

Backstitch, seeding stitch and split backstitch all have similar ways of working, yet each produces different results.

Backstitch (in lilac), seeding stitch (in dark green) and split backstitch (in yellow).

To start all three stitches...

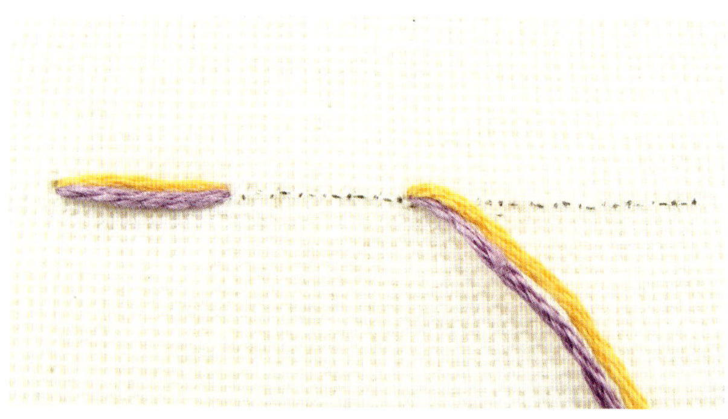

1 Start as if you were working running stitch (two different coloured threads are shown here for clarity).

2 For backstitch: take the needle down close to the previous stitch.

2 For seeding stitch: take the needle down halfway between the stitches.

2 For split backstitch: take the needle down between the strands of the previous stitch.

Backstitch

Backstitch is such a versatile stitch.

Regular backstitch is a line stitch.

Backstitch can also be worked as filling: arrange rows of backstitch in the way shown above, to make a pattern resembling brick stitch (the latter is not covered in this book).

Seeding stitch

Despite its resemblance to running stitch, seeding stitch can look nicer due to its rounded and well-anchored individual stitches. It's also known as isolated backstitch.

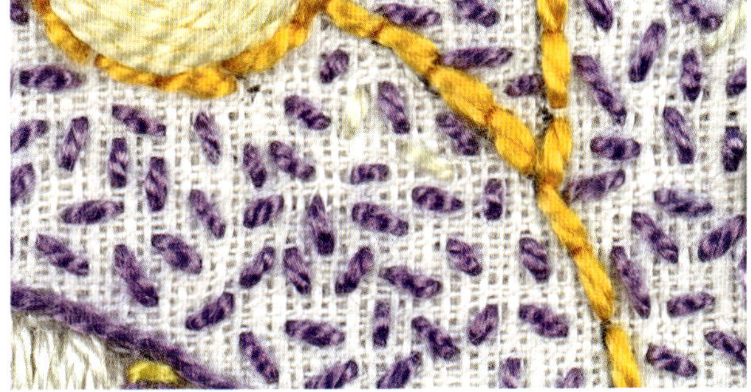

A mosaic-like effect, produced by scattering seeding stitches over the design area.

Split backstitch

Split backstitch looks like split stitch (see Going further on page 119), yet is far easier to work. Today we use split backstitch mostly as a line stitch, while centuries ago, in ecclesiastical embroidery, it was used as a filling stitch.

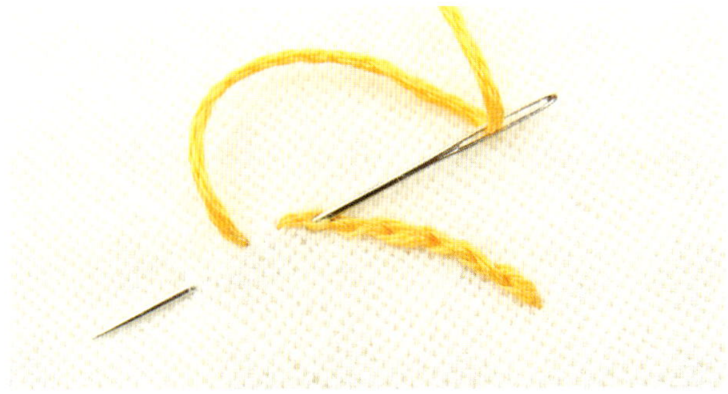

COUCHING

Couching means to stitch one thread in place using tiny tying stitches worked in another thread. The tying stitches create a decorative effect, being worked in the same or in a contrasting colour thread.

Prepare two threads: a heavier one – to be couched (which is called the *laid* thread), and a finer one for the tying stitches (also called the *tying* thread).

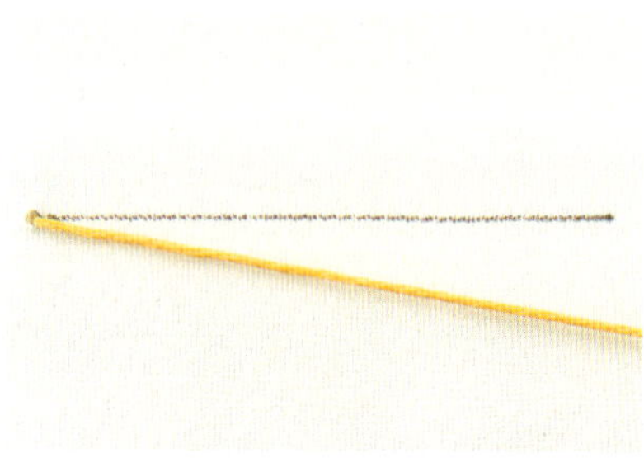

1 Bring the laid thread up at the beginning of a stitch line and unthread the needle to loosen the thread.

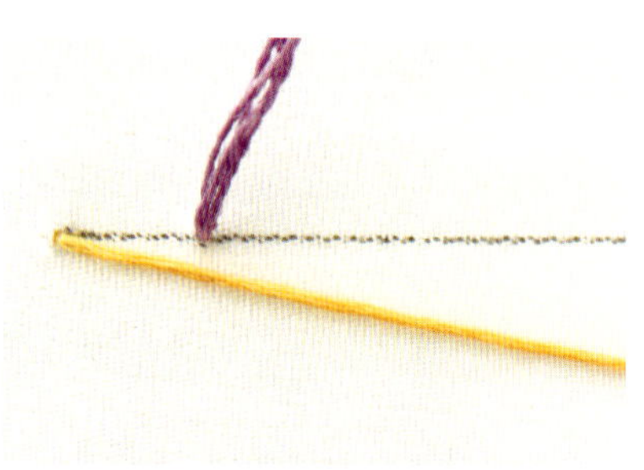

2 Come up with the tying thread.

3 Go down on the other side of the laid thread.

4 To make a tying stitch smaller, bring the needle down through the same hole in the fabric (or very close to the spot you went up through).

5 Continue working tying stitches: go over the laid thread and down to the back of the fabric.

6 Once all the laid thread is couched, bring both threads to the back of the fabric. Look at the two tying stitches on the right-hand end of the stitch line: they are longer than the others. This is optional; smaller stitches usually look nicer.

Couching as filling

To create a filling stitch, work rows of couching close together. This is also called Bokhara couching. You can arrange the tying stitches in a brickwork pattern, as shown on the right in lilac.

Optional: use double thread for the laid thread (as shown).

SATIN STITCH

There are two ways to work satin stitch: either cover both sides of the fabric (this is regular, or double-sided, satin stitch), or cover only the right side of the fabric with tiny stitches on the back (this is surface satin) – both look the same from the front of your work. Surface satin stitch is a way to save thread and to make the stitching less bulky.

Work straight stitches close to each other. Work left to right, to create the regular/double-sided satin stitch. Or, work one stitch left to right and the next stitch right to left to create surface satin stitch.

The front of the work: the top section is worked in double-sided satin stitch; the bottom section is worked in surface satin stitch. Both look the same from the front.

The back of the work: you can see the top section of double-sided satin stitch differs from the surface satin stitch at the bottom of the work.

WOVEN STITCHES

Woven wheel and woven filling are similar techniques. The difference in their appearance comes from the different arrangement of foundation stitches. The star pattern (see right, top) is the base for the wheel, and the vertical lines (see right, bottom) are the base for the woven filling. Whichever the foundation, make sure thread tails are nicely secured, otherwise the foundation stitches can get unpicked. Contrasting colours below are for clarity, but you can also play with colours for the benefit of your design.

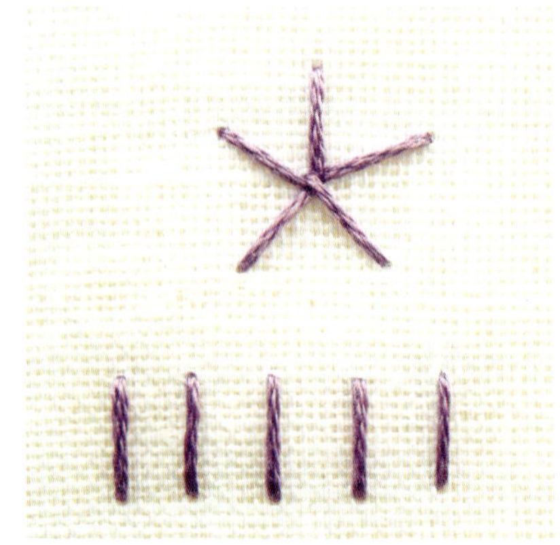

Woven wheel

Having worked the foundation star pattern, bring the needle up in the centre, work the weaving, and only go down when the foundation stitches are completely covered.

1 For the foundation, work five straight stitches, coming together in the centre. Weaving: the needle skips over one stitch of the foundation and passes under the next one. This is the Key Move.

2 The thread is shown loose for clarity. Tighten it every time you go under a stitch – but do not pull on it too much.

3 The pattern is beginning to form. The thread is shown loosely woven for you to see the alternation in over and under passes. Never leave it loose like this in your work – tighten it up as normal.

4 Progress. Cover all the foundation and then bring the needle to the back. The uncovered parts of the foundation are presented here for clarity – however, you may also wish to stop at this point.

The finished woven wheel.

Woven filling

Come up at the beginning of a row of weaving. Do the weaving. Go down at the end of the row. Come up for the next row close to the spot you went down through. Repeat. Choose threads for the foundation of the same colour as those for weaving. However, having practised the technique, play with colour for weaving, for example changing it for a contrasting or toning colour twice or three times as you progress.

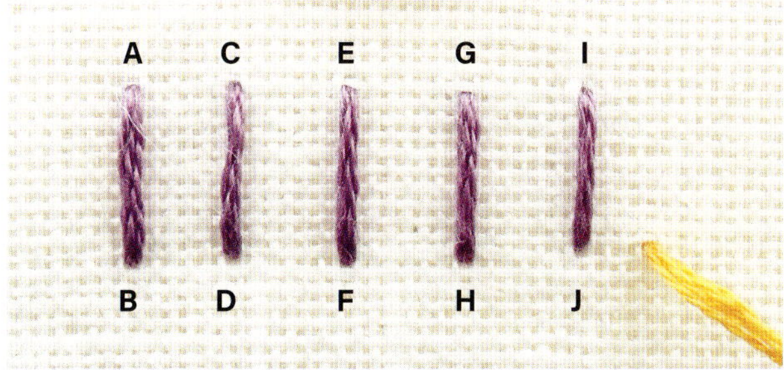

1 For the foundation, work equally spaced straight stitches, following the order suggested by the letters: come up at A, go down at B, come up at C, and so on. This way it is easier to keep the stitches parallel and nicely anchored. Remember to properly secure the thread at A and J, otherwise the foundation stitches may get unpicked. Next, bring up a blunt tapestry needle, threaded with the thread for weaving (yellow in the photograph).

2 The very first row is the simplest one: go over the first stitch of the foundation and under the second one. Repeat to the end of the row and go down.

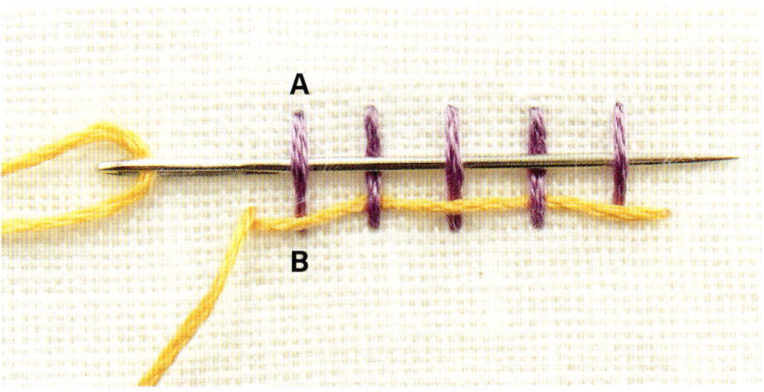

3 For the next row, come up close to where you went down. Now decide which way to pass the nearest stitch of the foundation. In the first row shown here, the weaving thread passed *over* stitch AB. Therefore, in the second row you go *under* stitch AB. Once you have figured this out, the rest is simple: weave, alternating the over and under passes of the needle, and go down at the end of the row.

4 To finish, continue the very same way, until all the foundation is covered. Always go down at the end of the finished row and come up next to it, to start a new row of weaving. Check whether to pass over or under the first stitch of the foundationn at the beginning of a new row.

Floral Butterfly

Some parts of this design resemble butterfly wings and antennae, as suggested in the name. Do you want to tell me there is no such flower in nature? That is why I love crewel patterns, as they allow all sorts of imaginary flora!

Notice how lovely it looks when satin stich is covered with lattice – this can also be a great way to hide any minor imperfections in satin stitches.

Satin stitch is worked here using the whole strand (six threads) of stranded cotton thread to make the surface elevated. The usual way is to stitch satin in one or two threads.

SIZE

12.5 x 15cm (5 x 6in)

MATERIALS

DMC pearl cotton thread, size 8 (P8):

52 variegated, light to dark shades of Lilac

725 Topaz

DMC pearl cotton thread, size 12 (P12):

3823 Yellow – ultra pale

Anchor pearl cotton thread, size 12 (P12A):

110 Lavender – very dark

DMC stranded cotton thread (SC):

818 Baby Pink

BLANC

3326 Rose – light

335 Rose

3345 Hunter Green – dark

PATTERN NOTES

You will see I have stitched some of the symmetrical zones in different ways or using different colours – you can choose to do this, or pick your favourite side and make your design totally symmetrical.

The instructions use some abbreviations of thread names, see page 24.

STITCHES USED

- Seeding stitch (line and filling), see page 60
- Backstitch (line and filling), see page 60
- Split backstitch, see page 60
- Couching, see page 62
- Satin stitch, see page 63
- Woven wheel, see page 64
- Woven filling, see page 65
- Straight stitch, see page 30
- Arrowhead stitch, see page 30
- Stem stitch, see page 33
- Lazy daisy stitch, see page 38
- Lattice, see page 42
- Fly stitch, see page 48
- Fly stitch leaf, see page 50
- Buttonhole stitch, see page 52

INSTRUCTIONS

Top part

1 Woven filling SC-818, 3326, 335(2), outlined in stem stitch P12-3823.

2 Woven wheel P12-3823, outlined in backstitch P8-725.

3 Backstitch P8-725.

4 Couching: laid thread P8-725, tying stitches SC-3345(2) (optional: work two tying stitches close to each other instead of the usual single stitch).
Inside the design area and right next to the couching, work a line of seeding stitch SC-3345(6).

5 Seeding stitch (filling) P12A-110; P12-3823.

6 Woven filling P8-52 outlined in stem stitch P12A-110.

7 Buttonhole stitch (light yellow) P12-3823 and couching (pink) SC-3326(6;2).

8 Straight stitches, radiating from the bottom of the area P8-725.

9 Satin stitch (off-white) SC-BLANC(6) covered with lattice (lilac) P12A-110 for lattice stitches and P8-725 for tying stitches.

10 Green: two rows of backstitch (filling) SC-3345(6). White: one row of couching: laid thread SC-BLANC(6), tying stitches P12A-110.

11 Cover the shape with fly stitch leaf (green) SC-3345(2), leaving small gaps between individual stitches. Then work a lazy daisy stitch (pale yellow) around each 'spike' of the fly stitches P12-3823. The leaf is outlined in backstitch, SC-3345(1).
Optional: fly stitch leaf on the right-hand side of this design is worked with individual fly stitches placed closer together than the left-hand side. Gaps are smaller and filled with straight stitches SC-335(2).

12 Seeding stitch (filling) SC-3345(2), outlined with stem stitch SC-3345(2) and one line of seeding stitch SC-3345(6).

13 Satin stitch P12-3823; outlined in stem stitch P12A-110, SC-335 and 3326(2).
Optional: the right-hand side of the pattern is worked in several rows of couching: use one or two threads of P8-725 as laid thread, and work tying stitches in P8-52.

TIP

'Transitional' rows for weaving

Three different coloured threads are used for the woven filling in step 1. To make the contrast less dramatic, work two 'transitional rows' of weaving before applying a new colour, that is rows worked in threads of two colours at the same time: one strand of the colour which has just been used and the other strand of a new colour.

1
2
3
4
5
6
7
8
9
10
11
12
13

Bottom part

1 Fly stitch leaf P8-52.

2 Arrowhead stitch (or three short lines of stem stitch) P8-52.

3 Split backstitch P8-52.

4 Satin stitch SC-BLANC.

5 Three lines of backstitch as filling SC-3345(6).

6 Buttonhole stitch P12-3823.

7 First work arrowhead stitches P8-52 (shown in green lines below) and then fill the gaps with fly stitches P12-3823 (shown in blue lines below).

8 Fly stitch leaf P8-52.

9 Woven filling P8-52.

10 Split stitch SC-3345(2).

11 Two lines of split backstitch SC-335; 818(2). Inside the area: three lines of seeding stitch SC-BLANC(6).

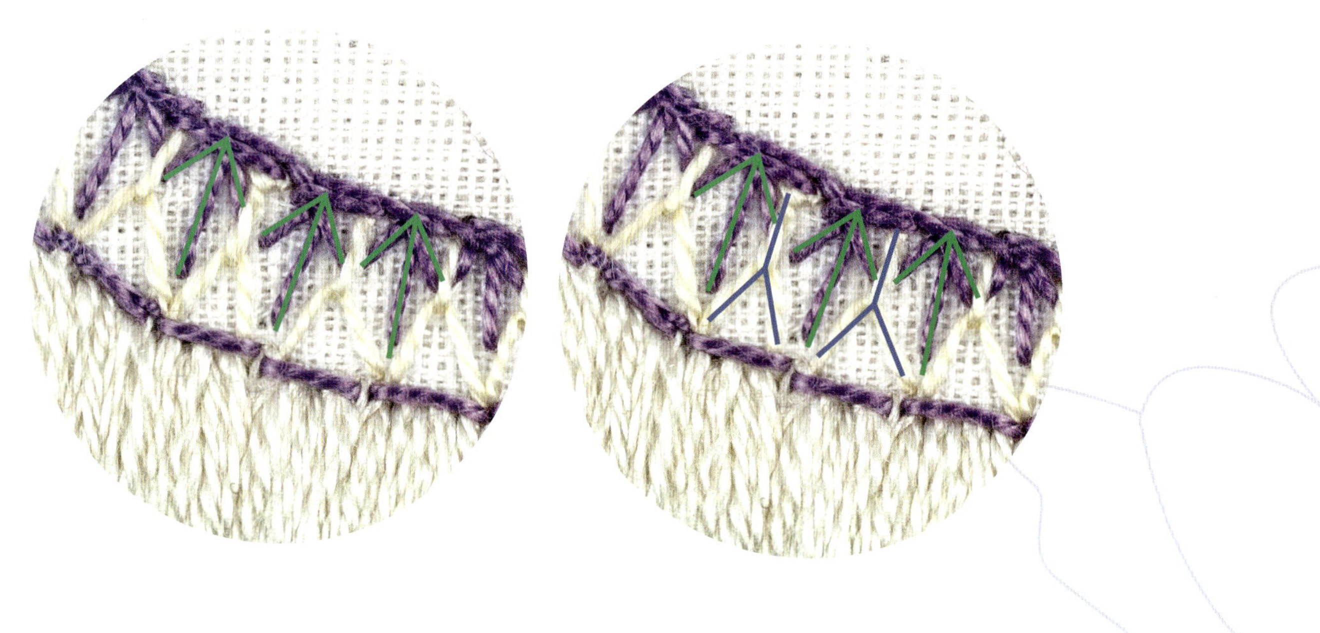

1
2
3
4
5
6
7
8
9
10
11

Techniques

FERN STITCH

Two threads of contrasting colour are used here for clarity. Work all the fern stitches using the same thread.

1 Work an arrowhead stitch (see page 30) at the tip of a stitch line. Add one more arrowhead right below.

2 Note the direction of stitching on the left side of the stitch.

3 Work a stitch on the right, following the same direction: from the outside towards the place where all the three stitches come together.

4 Continue the same way to create a line of fern stitch. Also try variegated thread for this stitch, for an interesting effect.

LAID WORK

Laid work resembles couching worked over satin stitch. You could use either the same or a different colour thread for each of the three steps.

1 Work an area of surface satin stitch (see page 63).

2 Add the laid thread: straight stitches, perpendicular to the surface satin stitches.

3 Try to keep the intervals between stitches consistent.

4 Work tying stitches, arranged in a brickwork pattern. Use finer thread to create smaller stitches.

The finished laid work.

RAISED STEM STITCH

This is the very same stem stitch shown on page 33, only it is worked over a foundation, which means the work is done on the right side of the fabric, and the needle passes through the fabric only to start and finish a stitch line. Apply the River Bank Rule (see top of page 33) to get the desired look for the stitch.

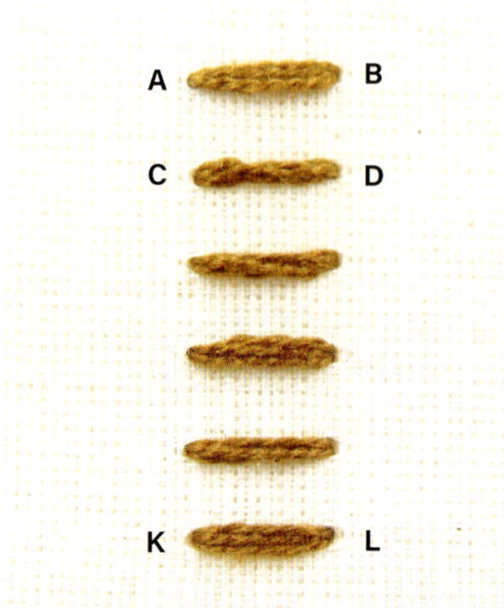

Foundation

Work evenly spaced straight stitches: for doodle stitching, arrange them as a ladder (see photograph), but to embroider a design, work them across the stitching area. Anchor the thread securely at A and L.

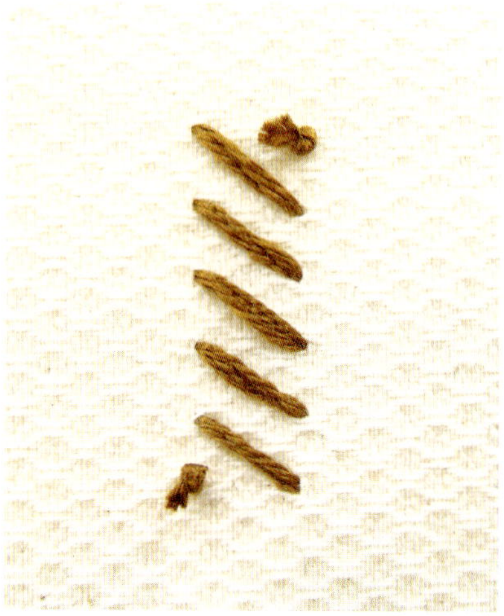

The back of the foundation stitches.

Do not change thread for stitching; contrasting colours are used here for clarity.

1 To start the first stitch line, come up through the fabric and go around the nearest stitch of the foundation. Remember to place the loop to the right side.

2 The result.

3 Continue working: the loop goes over the right side.

4 To finish the first stitch line, bring the needle down.

5 To start the second stitch line, come up close to the spot you went down. Go around the nearest stitch of the foundation, placing the loop to the right side. Yes, the right is not a misprint here: define sides, based on the direction of stitching, and that direction has been changed.

6 Proceed the same way. Go down at the end of the stitch line (not shown).

7 Work as many stitch lines as needed to cover the foundation. For a more voluminous look of raised stem, work a few more lines, compared to what is shown in the photograph.

Raised stem stitch – knit variation

1 For the knit variation, work one stitch line with loops placed over the right side and the next line with loops over the left. Continue alternating lines, till all the foundation is covered.

2 Contrasting threads show the odd and even rows, but you can use the same colour thread in your work.

TIP

For either variation of raised chain stitch, avoid pulling on the thread too tightly, or the foundation stitches may get distorted.

FRENCH KNOT, PISTIL STITCH AND FRENCH KNOT – LOOSE

These three stitches have a lot in common, so it is easier to learn them together. They all share the same starting point but, due to the slight variations, each results in a different look.

The starting point for all three stitches:

1 The starting point resembles a letter 'T'.

2 Wrap the thread around the needle two or three times (twice in the photograph).

French knot

Continuing from steps 1 and 2 above, work steps 3 and 4 below to create a French knot.

3 Tighten all the wraps and go down close to the initial hole.

4 Take the needle to the back of the fabric and you will end up with a French knot.

Pistil stitch

Continuing from steps 1 and 2 opposite, work steps 3 and 4 below to create pistil stitch, also known as tailed knot.

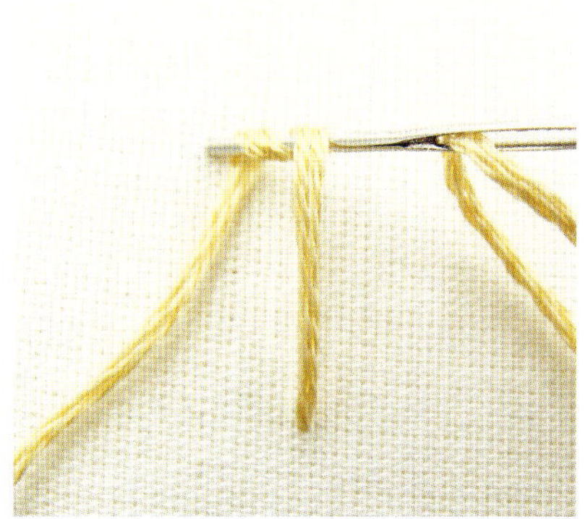

3 Tighten all the wraps and go down away from the initial hole.

4 Take the needle to the back of the fabric and you will end up with pistil stitch.

French knot – loose

Continuing from steps 1 and 2 opposite, work steps 3 and 4 below to create a loose French knot – you can see in the photos how this differs from a regular French knot.

3 Do not tighten the wraps, and take the needle down close to the initial hole.

4 Take your needle to the back of the fabric and you will end up with a loose French knot.

TIP

To easily keep the wraps loose, follow the pistil stitch steps, *but* do not go down that far. Instead, drag the needle tip along the right side of the fabric all the way to the initial hole, pressing on the untightened wraps with your finger. Now go down and you will see a small ring formed from the 'tail' of pistil stitch.

Snowdrop Swirl

The curved lines of this design resemble patterns of Elizabethan crewel embroidery. A snowdrop flower, a bud, a leaf and a stem are the main elements, repeatedly scattered around the design, therefore providing wider practice in stitching.

To stitch the swirl on white fabric, you may wish to make the flower petals blue, to contrast with the background. This way you will create the swirl of Scilla (or squill), which is another early spring bloom.

SIZE

17.5 x 13cm (7 x 5in)

THREADS

DMC pearl cotton thread, size 8 (P8):

105 Variegated Brown

94 Variegated Olive

3345 Hunter Green – dark

BLANC

DMC stranded cotton thread (SC):

3345 Hunter Green – dark

BLANC

PATTERN NOTES

The original stitching calls for variegated threads with shades and colours varying along the thread – choose appropriate sections of these threads to produce the look you like.

The instructions use some abbreviations of thread names, see page 24.

STITCHES USED

- Fern stitch, see page 72
- Laid work, see page 73
- Raised stem stitch, see page 74
- Raised stem stitch – knit, see page 75
- French knot, see page 76
- French knot – loose, see page 77
- Straight stitch, see page 30
- Outline stitch, see page 33
- Stem stitch (line and filling), see page 33
- Granitos, see page 51
- Split backstitch, see page 61
- Surface satin stitch, see page 63

INSTRUCTIONS

Sequence of work

Option 1 Work the flowers first, then the leaves and stems. Finish with the patches of snow at the bottom of the design. Pros: you will get more experienced in a particular stitch, while working it over and over again. Cons: ensure your hands are clean as you start stitching the greenery, so as not to make the white flower petals grey.

Option 2 Work from top to bottom (as if following the imaginary vertical columns or horizontal rows). This is the typical way of stitching larger designs, as it prevents you from rubbing your hands against the finished part of the embroidery.

Elements of the design

The following are worked in the same manner all over the design.

1 Flat flower petals. Choose one of the following techniques:
- **a** Satin stitch P8-BLANC.
- **b** Laid work P8-BLANC for the foundation and SC-BLANC(1) for the laid thread and tying stitches.

2 Three-dimensional flower petals and the bud. Choose one of the following techniques:
- **a** Raised stem stitch P8-BLANC.
- **b** Raised stem stitch – knit P8-BLANC.

3 Petal outline. Choose one of the following techniques:
- **a** Stem stitch SC-3345(1).
- **b** Outline stitch SC-3345(1).

4 Stamens: granitos P8-3345. Depending on the size of the flower, work two, three or four straight stitches for one granitos.

5 Flower cup: straight stitches P8-3345. Radiate these stitches from the tip of the flower cup.

6 Stems: choose one of the following techniques:
- **a** Stem stitch P8-94; P8-105; P8-3345.
- **b** Split backstitch P8-94; P8-105; P8-3345.

7 Leaves: stem stitch filling P8-94; P8-105; P8-3345.

8 Growth at the bottom: choose one of the following techniques:
- **a** Fern stitch P8-94; P8-105; P8-3345.
- **b** Split backstitch P8-94; P8-105; P8-3345.

9 Snow patches: choose one of the following techniques:
- **a** French knot and French knot – loose. Play with the number of wraps (one, two or three). P8-BLANC; SC-BLANC(1 or 2).
- **b** Raised stem stitch – knit P8-BLANC.

5
3
7
2b
4
1b
6
2a
7
8a
8b
9a
9b

Techniques

WOVEN BAR LEAF

I have adapted the woven bar stitch (not in this book) to the shape of a small leaf. Contrasting thread is used for clarity: you can use the same thread for all the steps. Try variegated thread; it will make the stitched leaf look more natural. With stranded cotton, consider the size of a leaf when you decide on the number of threads for stitching. If in doubt, do some test stitching first.

1 Foundation: work two loops of chain stitch, with the top one being very small (shown in coral).

2 Come up inside the loop, bring the needle over and under the right-hand side of the loop and pull the needle through. This is step 1 of the Key Move.

3 Do not bring the needle to the back of the fabric. Instead, go over and under the left-hand side of the loop. This is step 2 of the Key Move.

4 Continue working the Key Move until the whole leaf shape is covered with weaving.

The finished stitch.

SATIN STITCH LEAF

A simple, pretty stitch that looks more complex than it is!

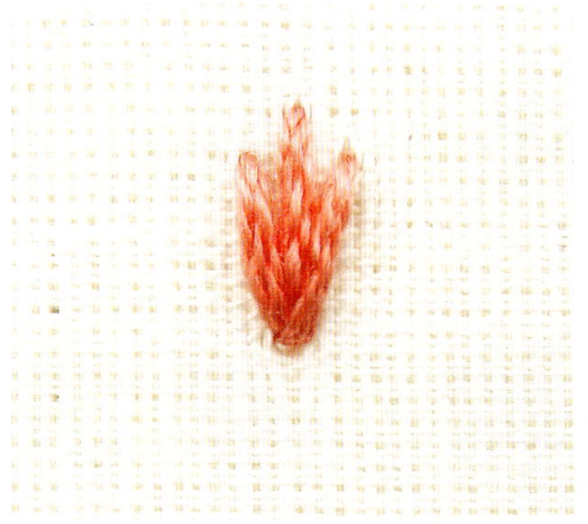

1 Start with arrowhead stitch (see page 30).

2 Key Move, step 1: work a straight stitch on the left.

3 Key Move, step 2: work a straight stitch on the right, coming down through the same hole.

4 Repeat the Key Move, working pairs of stitches. Remember to bring the right and left stitch of each pair through the same hole in fabric.

5 Add more straight stitches. The trick is to work them in pairs.

The finished leaves. Contrasting threads are for clarity, but it is worth trying variegated thread for a great effect!

CRETAN STITCH LEAF

Various colours are shown here for clarity; do not change thread as you stitch. I took the liberty of introducing some new points to assist you in mastering this charming technique: note the line drawings below.

Preparation

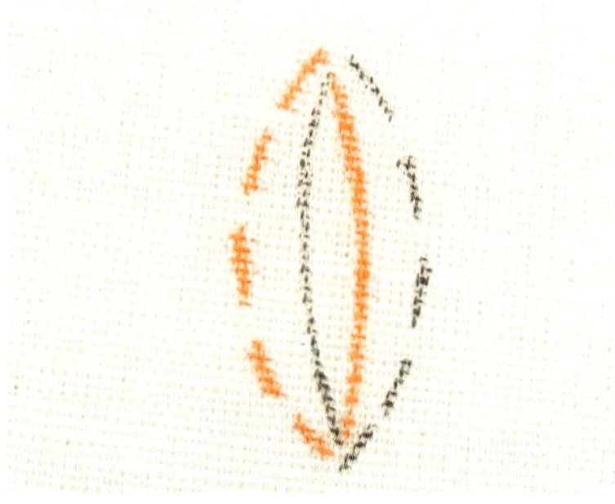

1 Either draw, or imagine, the lines shown. As you stitch, first come up on the solid black line and go down via the dashed black line. Next, come up on the solid orange line and go down via the orange dashed line. Repeat. Remember to go down on dashed lines and 'pair up' lines of the same colour.

Stitching

2 The tip of the leaf is the only tricky part in Cretan stitch, therefore I suggest working it in tulip stitch (page 40).

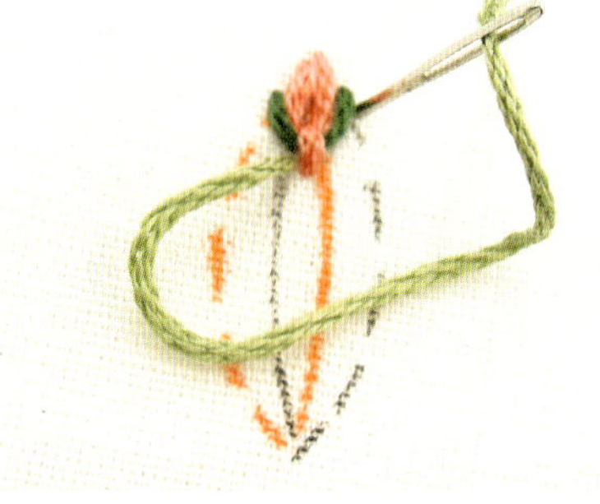

3 Work a straight stitch through the black lines. Do not tighten it to form a loop.

4 Come up inside the loop.

5 Tighten up the loop.

6 Work a straight stitch through the orange lines. Do not tighten it to form a loop.

7 Come up inside the loop. Tighten up the loop (not shown in the photograph for clarity).

8 Continue working stitches via the black lines, then via the orange lines. The stitches in the photograph are spaced a little for clarity.

The finished Cretan leaf: a nice braid shows up along the midrib (the leaf on the left). Contrasting colours highlight individual stitches (the leaf on the right).

CATERPILLAR (SATIN THREADED CHAIN STITCH)

The thread of the lacing (shown in coral) 'hangs' on the loops of the chain stitch (shown in green). Use either one or two thread colours for your stitching.

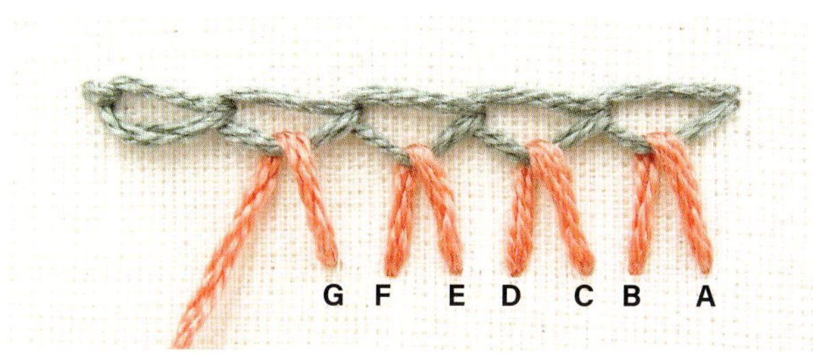

The regular order of stitching (marked in lettering): come up at A, bring the needle through the first loop of the chain, go down at B. Come up at C. Repeat to the end of the line.

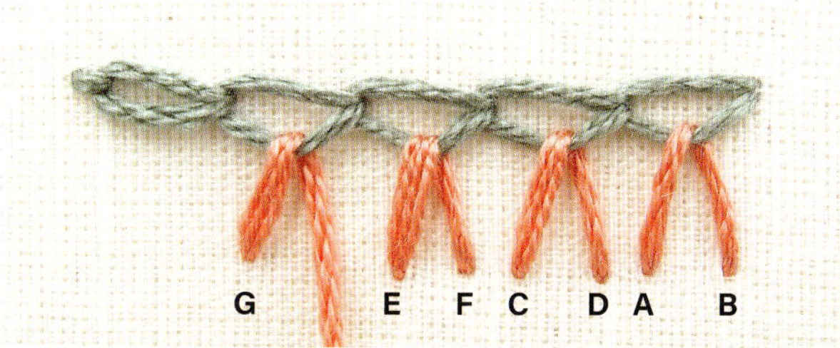

The alternative order of stitching. Sometimes this is worth observing to make the supporting stitches longer and therefore to better anchor the stitches.

TIP

This stitch creates an intricate filling pattern. It is easier to work all the lines of chain stitch before the lacing (as shown in pink thread in the photograph on the left).

RIBBED WHEEL

Contrasting threads are shown below for clarity, but you can vary thread colours as you wish – for example, work three rounds in pink, then change to white and finally a few rounds in red – to make concentric circles of different colours. Toning threads also work nicely!

1 Foundation: either follow the steps shown on page 64, or work the foundation as shown in the photograph, with a cluster of French knots in the centre. Remember to secure foundation stitches nicely, and vary their number, depending on the size of your circle.

2 Bring the thread up close to the centre. Remember to work all the whipping detached from the fabric and only go down once the whole wheel is filled. The very first move is unique: pass underneath *one* stitch of the foundation.

3 The technique suggests bringing the needle *under*, *over*, and once more *under* each stitch of the foundation. Yet it is never performed in the way shown here. There is a better way, shown in the next photograph.

4 Here is a better and quicker way to perform the under-over-under movement. Can you spot the difference with what is shown in the previous photograph? Yes, that is it: the needle is brought under two stitches in one go. This is the Key Move.

5 Repeat the Key Move until all the foundation stitches are covered with whipping (incomplete in the photograph), then bring the needle to the back of the fabric.

RIBBED FILLING

The whipping method here is identical to the one opposite, but the foundation stitches are arranged in a different way. Remember to come up at the beginning of each line, and go down at the end of each line of whipping. Also remember to securely anchor the first and the last stitches of the foundation, or they can come unpicked.

1 To start a line, pass the needle under *one* stitch of the foundation.

2 Key Move: go under *two* stitches – the one that you are whipping and the next one.

3 Repeat the Key Move to the end of the line, bringing the needle under two stitches in one go.

4 Go down at the end of the line. Come up to start a new line.

5 To start, go under just one stitch of the foundation (similar to the first line). Proceed, working the Key Move (passing the needle under *two* stitches in one go). Repeat to the end of the line, then go down.

6 Repeat to cover the foundation stitches (the photograph shows the incomplete ribbed filling for clarity: a few more lines of whipping are needed).

Peony

Due to the amazing work of plant breeders, none of us can nowadays complain of our poor skills in drawing flowers, for if you are unhappy with your drawing of a tulip, you can search for its varieties and no doubt you will find the proper cultivar which resembles your tulip both in shape and colour! And that is exactly what happened to my peony: meet the Coral Charm cultivar!

The design shows a great selection of stitching techniques for all kinds of leaves, from the tiniest ones to the largest – all of them suitable for beginners. Practise your stitches on a spare piece of fabric before working the design, and remember to try these techniques to work berries or flower petals in your future designs.

SIZE

21 x 16cm (8¼ x 6¼in)

THREADS

DMC pearl cotton thread, size 8 (P8):

937 Avocado Green – medium

351 Coral

352 Coral – light

DMC pearl cotton thread, size 12 (P12):

3865 Winter White

Anchor pearl cotton thread, size 12 (P12A):

009 Coral – light

256 Olive

DMC stranded cotton thread (SC):

3345 Hunter Green – dark

4045 Variegated Green

PATTERN NOTES

Note the two suggested ways of working caterpillar (see page 85), and apply one or the other of them, depending on the space available for stitching. Our goal is to make supporting stitches long enough to hold the stitching on the right side of the fabric in place.

The instructions use some abbreviations of thread names, see page 24.

STITCHES USED

- Woven bar leaf, see page 82
- Satin stitch leaf, see page 83
- Cretan stitch leaf, see page 84
- Caterpillar, see page 85
- Ribbed wheel, see page 86
- Ribbed filling, see page 87
- Running stitch, see page 32
- Stem or outline stitch, see page 33
- Chain stitch, see page 39
- Lattice, see page 42
- Granitos, see page 51
- Blanket stitch, see page 52
- Buttonholed chain stitch, see page 53
- Split backstitch, see page 60
- Couching, see page 62
- Satin stitch, see page 63
- Raised stem stitch, see page 74
- French knot, see page 76
- Pistil stitch, see page 77

INSTRUCTIONS

Outer petals and centre of the peony

Areas 1a and 1b are covered with lattice. **Optional:** it is easier to work lattice over all the three areas (1a, 1b, and 3) – as shown in pink in the illustration below – as if they were a single area. Of course, we do not want any lattice in area 3, but this time it is all right: the thread used for lattice is very fine and will therefore not create an obsticle for embroidering area 3. Ensure that your fabric is tightly stretched in your embroidery hoop before you start working lattice.

Lattice: P12-3865.

1a Tying stitches in P12-3865.

1b Tying stitches in P12A-009.

Then embellish zone 1a with French knots around the intersections of the lattice: two knots in P12A-256 and two in P8-937.

Petal tips

2a Raised stem stitch P12-3865.

2b Buttonholed chain in either P8-351 or P12A-009.

2c Stem stitch in either P8-351 or P12A-009.

Inside petals

3 Satin stitch P8-352. Outline each petal in stem stitch P12A-009.

Stem

4 Raised stem stitch SC-3345(2).

Two huge leaves

5a Midrib in chain stitch P8-937.

5b Fill in the leaves using satin threaded chain stitch, alternating rows in P8-937; SC-4045(2); P12-3865.

5c Couching: laid thread SC-3345(6), tying stitches P12A-009.

2a
2b
2c
1a
3
1b
5c
4
5b
5a

Medium-sized leaves

Leaves of 7a type
Ovals: granitos P12A-256.
Petiole: straight stitch P12A-009.
Midrib and outline: stem stitch P12A-009, P12A-256, SC-4045(2).

Leaves of 7b type
Filling for the halves of the leaf: running stitch P12A-009 and pistil stitch SC-3345(2).
Midrib and outline: stem stitch P12A-256, SC-4045(2).

Leaves of 7c type
Filling for one half of the leaf: ribbed filling SC-4045(2), with split stitch P12-3865 around it. Outline: stem stitch P8-937.

Braided midrib leaves

8 Cretan stitch leaf. Assorted green thread SC(2).

Smaller leaves

9 Satin stitch leaf, assorted green thread: SC(1) for the smaller leaves and SC(2) for the others.

Tiny leaves

10 Woven bar leaf SC-4045(2).

Laced leaf

11 Work buttonhole stitch, starting the individual stitches from the same hole in the fabric to give you a scallop shape. The whole leaf is worked in these scallops. Use P12A-256 on the left of the midrib and SC-4045(2) on the right.

Dotted outline leaf

12 Cover each half of the leaf with satin stitch P12-3865. Midrib is worked in couching: laid thread SC-3345(6), tying stitches SC-3345(1). Outlines are also worked in couching: laid thread SC-3345(6), tying stitches P12A-009.

Tendrils and stems

13 Split backstitch, stem stitch or outline stitch in assorted green threads.

7b
8
7a
11
10
13
12
6
9

Techniques

SILK SHADING

Silk shading may require some practice, but it is such a satifying stitch once you have got the hang of it! Let's practise on a flower petal, but you can apply this technique to any design area. To practise using one thread of stranded cotton, draw a petal approximately 1.5 x 1cm (¾ x ½in) on your fabric.

Preparatory work

SELECTING THREADS

Decide on the number of colours you'd like to use for shading, making sure they show visible contrast with one another. Decide whether you want the tip of a petal to be darker or lighter, and arrange the colour shades accordingly.

In the steps shown, the outer part of the petal is stitched in dark pink (colour 1), the middle part in mid-pink (colour 2), and the inside part in pale pink (colour 3).

For clarity, all the stitching was done in heavier thread than is usual for this technique. Therefore, no double thread has been used. For the actual stitching, use a double thread of stranded cotton to work the outer row, and a single thread for the rest of the shading.

GUIDING LINES

The direction of stitching is marked in pink lines and the borders of the colour zones in blue (as shown on the right) – think of the parallels and meridians of the globe. Either draw or imagine these lines: they are to guide your stitching. It is okay to spread a particular colour zone, or do another small alteration, if the process of stitching suggests it.

AWAY WASTE KNOT

The best approach with silk shading is to always start a new thread with a temporary knot, placed on the right side of the fabric, away from the area you are stitching. Having finished the thread, trim off the knot and the thread tail on the back. Perfectionists can, of course, go the super-secure way, and bring that thread tail underneath stitching on the back, before trimming off the excess thread. Yet, since the stitching of silk shading is very dense, such precautions are needless. What is needed is to protect the fabric against thread fibres, and to place the 'away waste knot' within another stitching area, so that the spot is to be covered with some stitching.

GUIDING WALL

Work split backstitch (see page 60) along the outlines – either all around the petal, or just along the edges you want to make elevated (in the photograph). This stitch also helps make the edge of a petal nicely rounded. Use a double thread in colour number 1 to work split backstitch.

Top to bottom: guiding lines; an away waste knot; guiding wall.

The stitching

It is easier for beginners to work silk shading in several journeys: stitch the area left to right, leaving gaps between stitches. Then go right to left, filling in these gaps. Make any number of these journeys, depending on your experience and the size of the area. As you become more experienced, you may prefer to stitch in one journey; yet, some embroiderers follow the 'journey' way of stitching forever, finding it more convenient and safer, since it helps to place each stitch at the proper angle, and prevents stitches from becoming overcrowded.

Outer row

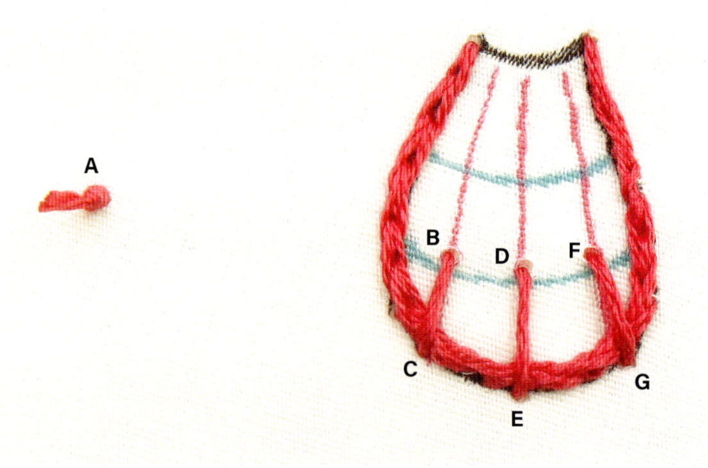

1 First journey: the outer row is the only row of silk shading when a double thread is used (ignore the single thread in the photograph, it is for clarity). Work in colour number 1. Bring the needle down at A for the away waste knot. Come up at B, inside the petal. Go down at C, outside the petal, and over the line of split backstitch. Your stitching is supposed to cover the split backstitch! Come up at D, go down at E. Make as many stitches as you wish (there are three stitches in the photograph).

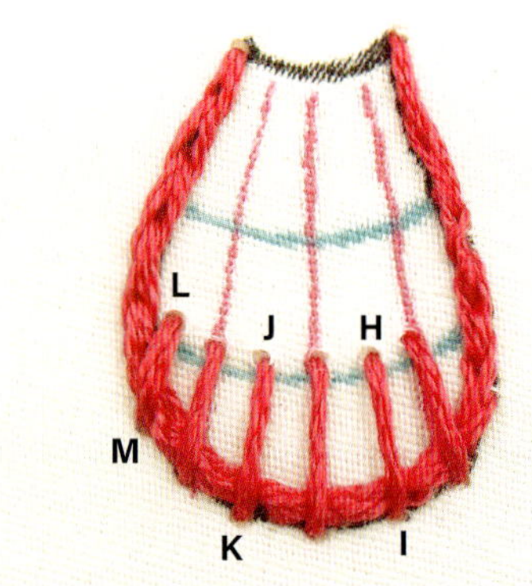

2 Second journey: using the same thread add a stitch or two inside each gap. For each stitch, come up inside the petal, and go down outside the petal. Follow the order marked H–M.

3 Third journey: fill in the gaps with more stitching.

4 The last journey: fill in all the remaining gaps. Do as many journeys as you need. Practise to find out how many journeys work best for you.

Middle row

Remember to start every new thread with an away waste knot.

1 Making a start: stitch in a single thread of colour 2. To start a new stitch, bring the needle up *through* the stitches of the previous row. That is the rule for all the remaining rows of shading; it helps to hide the border between rows.

2 Work in journeys again: it helps to focus on the direction of stitching.

Last row

Remember to start every new thread with an away waste knot.

1 Making a start: stitching in a single thread of colour 3, and come up *through* the stitches of the previous row.

2 Work in journeys again: as your skill builds, you may want to work without an outline guide, but it still helps elevate the petal edge.

The finished silk shading. It does not look as nice as it might, because a heavy thread was used for stitching (for clarity). For the best result, always use one thread of stranded cotton or any other fine thread.

VERMICELLI STITCH

Vermicelli stitch is a variation of couching in curved patterns, formed by a travelling thread stitched down by tying stitches. Having brought the laid thread to the right side of the fabric, unthread its needle, or let it rest on a needle minder so that it does not interfere with your stitching of the tying thread.

Refer to couching on page 62 for the technique, but place the laid thread meandering across the stitching area. Use finer thread for the tying stitches.

TIP

Take inspiration from the pattern of a 'meandering river'! The word 'to meander' comes from the name of the river in West Asia, famous for its winding watercourse.

WHIPPED STITCHES – BACKSTITCH, SPLIT BACKSTITCH AND STEM STITCH

Work in the same way as for whipped running stitch to whip rows backstitch (page 61), split backstitch (page 60) and stem stitch (page 33). Whether you whip left to right or vice versa, makes no difference to the look of the finished stitch.

Vermicelli stitch is used in the Fuchsia project overleaf to create a beautiful texture on the sepals.

Fuschia

Silk shading has long been considered one of the most complex embroidery techniques. Luckily, nowadays beginners can enjoy stitching in silk shading, due to the clever range of tips and tricks which help with mastering the technique.

Fuchsias grow in a vast variety of colours – would you like to replace the colours of threads shown here to stitch your favourite cultivar?

SIZE

17.5 x 12.5cm (6¾ x 5in)

MATERIALS

DMC pearl cotton thread, size 8 (P8):

48 Variegated, shades of pink
605 Cranberry – very light

DMC pearl cotton thread, size 12 (P12):

524 Fern Green – very light

DMC stranded cotton thread (SC):

580 Moss Green - dark
936 Avocado Green – very dark
934 Black Avocado Green - dark
3865 Winter White
761 Salmon – light
3354 Dusty Rose – light
3733 Dusty Rose
3731 Dusty Rose – very dark
326 Rose – very dark
498 Christmas Red – dark

PATTERN NOTES

The right and left sides of the design have some small variations in the stitching and colours. You can choose to follow the instructions to make yours vary too, or choose the side you like most and repeat it on the other side of the design.

The instructions use some abbreviations of thread names, see page 24.

STITCHES USED

- Silk shading, see page 94
- Vermicelli stitch, see page 98
- Whipped stem stitch, see page 98
- Straight stitch, see page 30
- Whipped running stitch, see page 32
- Stem stitch (line and filling), see page 33
- Whipped chain – one side, see page 41
- Lattice, see page 42
- Fly stitch – leaf, see page 50
- Granitos, see page 51
- Split backstitch, see page 60
- Couching (line and filling), see page 62
- Woven wheel, see page 64
- Fern stitch, see page 72
- Raised stem stitch, see page 74
- French knot, see page 76

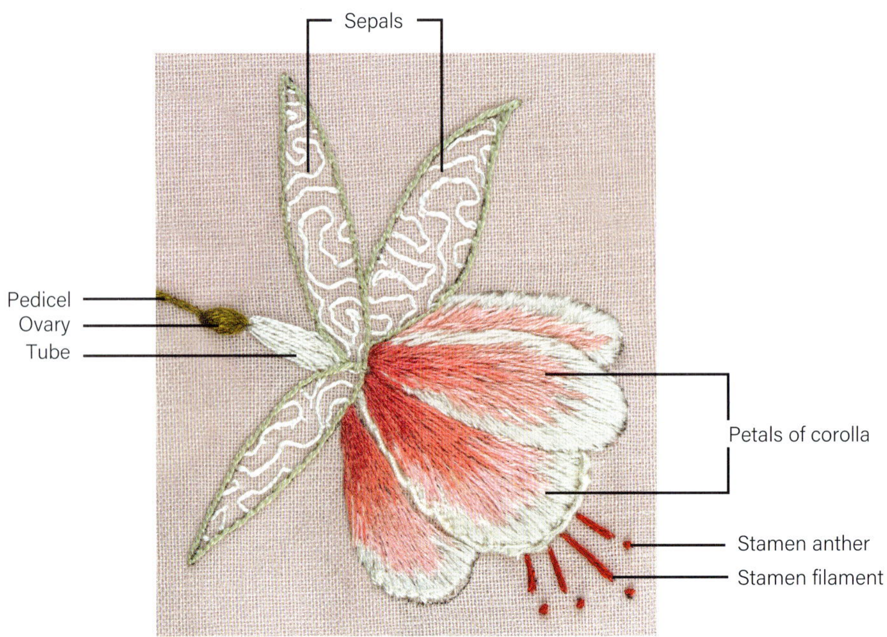

The parts of a fuschia flower.

INSTRUCTIONS

Flowers in full bloom

1 The right-hand flower:

Petals of corolla: first outline each petal in split backstitch, using SC-3865(2) and then work silk shading, applying SC-3865(2) along the outer edge, and then SC-761; 3354; 3733; 3731(1).

Optional: one of the petals in the photograph has been outlined in chain stitch with one side whipped. If you wish, try this for your stitching: outline the petal in chain stitch, whip the outer side of the chain, and cover the inner side of it with the first row of silk shading.

Sepals: vermicelli stitch SC-3865(2;1), outlined in stem stitch P12-524.

Tube: stem stitch filling SC-3865(2).

Ovary: granitos SC-580(2).

Pedicel: stem stitch SC-580(2).

Stamens: straight stitch P8-48 for filaments and French knots P8-48 for anthers.

Optional: the left-hand flower: a different colour scheme has been applied, and the techniques are mostly the same with some small variations mentioned below (see the photograph on the next page).

Petals of corolla: a different stitch for each petal, so that the two central petals look more dimensional: raised stem stitch, stem stitch filling with lattice on top of it, couching as filling, stem stitch filling P8-605.

Sepals: vermicelli stitch P8-48, tying stitches SC-498(1). Outline each sepal in couching P8-48, tied with SC-498(1).

Tube: silk shading SC-326; 3733; 3354(1)

Flower buds

2 Woven wheel: stem stitch P8-48. Work the wheel and stem stitch using contrasting shades of this variegated thread. **Optional:** left-hand flower bud. Fly stitch leaf P8-48. You can also add some lines in stem stitch, using the same thread.

2
2
1

Leaves

Some leaves in this design are completely covered with stitching; others have only been partly worked.

3a Shaded leaves: silk shading assorted green SC(1).

3b Leaves with stitched veins: fern stitch assorted green SC(2).

3c Transparent leaves with the midrib only: stem stitch assorted SC(2).

Twigs

4 Fern stitch assorted green SC(2).

Outlines of the heart

5 Stem stitch SC-943(2).

3a
3a
3b
4
3c
5

Techniques

PEKINESE STITCH

Work a line of backstitch (see page 60) and then lace it, using either the same or a contrasting thread.

1 Bring the needle underneath the second stitch of backstitch.

2 Having changed the direction, bring the needle underneath the first stitch. This forms a kind of wrapping around the joint of two stitches: this is the Key Move. Apply it to every joint along the backstitch.

3 Go down at the end (the last loop is untightened in the photograph).

BUTTONHOLE BLOCK SHADING

Shading of all sorts is quite a stitch family, which is popular in crewel embroidery. Several rows of buttonhole (shown incomplete in the photographs below) are worked next to each other, using contrasting thread colours.

1 Work the outer row (pale yellow) first.

2 Add the next row above.

3 Add the final row (for your stitching, stitch to the end of each row).

BATTLEMENT COUCHING

Lattice grids are worked almost on top of each other. Use thread of a new colour for each layer of the grid. You can also create cells of a diamond shape, which gives an interesting result.

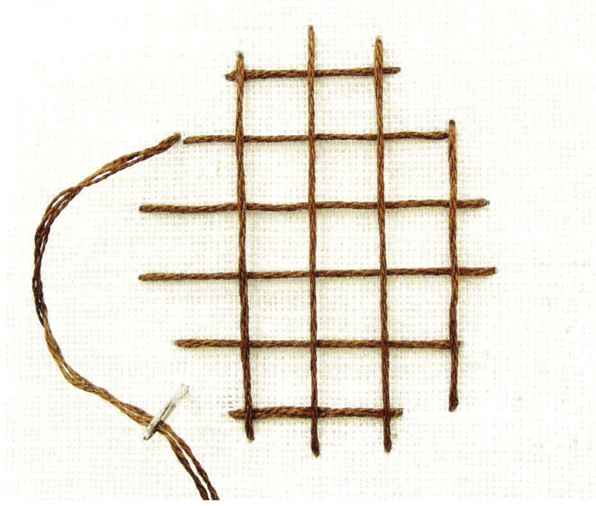

1 The first lattice: note that the vertical stitches go *over* the horizontal stitches.

2 The second lattice. Vertical stitches go *over* the horizontal stitches again. Also mind the shift in placement of the second lattice, compared to that of the first lattice.

3 The third lattice: work another layer of the pattern, again putting the needle in a fraction above the previous layer. The vertical goes over the horizontal again. Up to seven layers of lattice is possible, but three to five is ideal.

4 Anchor the intersections of the top lattice only, using finer thread.

DETACHED BUTTONHOLE – CORDED

A lovely stitch family, based on detached buttonhole stitches (DB stitches), is known as needle lace. This variation is called 'corded' because stitches are worked over the core thread.

Work DB stitches using a blunt-tipped tapestry needle, so as not to pierce the threads. Alternatively, continue using a sharp-tipped chenille needle, but take the needle eye through the stitches first. Once finished, outline the area in stem stitch.

The pattern is so intricate – the contrasting threads shown below are to clarify each step; in your own work, use the same colour thread for all steps.

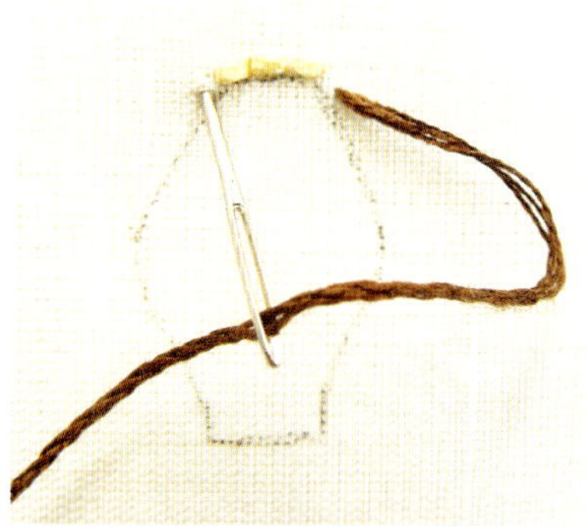

1 Preparation: work backstitch (yellow) along the part of the shape that looks flat. Then add a straight stitch (brown), to form the core thread.

2 Key Move: add a DB stitch (orange). Note that all DB stitches of the first row are attached *to the backstitch.*

3 Continue to the end of the row, then go down (not shown).

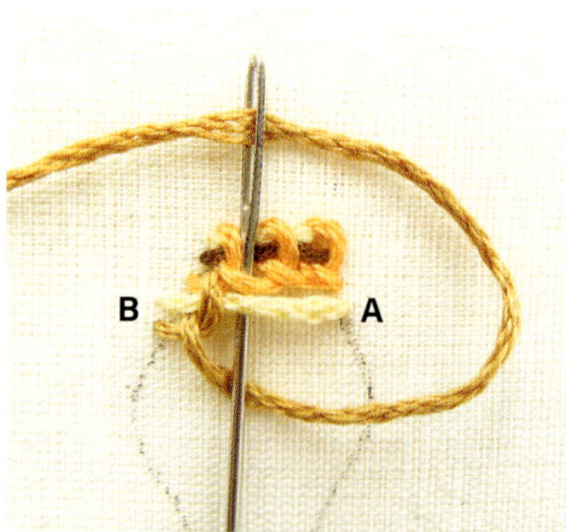

4 For the second row, come up at A and go down at B to lay a core thread (yellow). Work DB stitches (beige), this time attaching them *to the first row of DB.*

5 Note: there are four DB stitches in this row (while in the previous row there were only three). This is to follow the widening in the shape of the area. Always add a stitch or two at the sides of a row to increase and skip over a stitch or two to decrease.

6 Come up and work a straight stitch for the third row (brown). Work DB stitches (yellow), attaching them *to the DB of the second row*. Always attach DB to the stitches of the previous row.

7 At the end of each row, go to the back of the fabric. Then bring the needle up 1mm from this spot (not shown here) to lay the core thread.

8 End with tying stitches (brown), to attach the last row of DB to the fabric. Outline the area in stem stitch (not shown).

9 Do not be confused if your needle lace tends to shrink as you work DB. The tying stitches will make the lace stretch out properly.

Sunrise Singer

Birds are often used for crewel designs, and here is a twittering bird on a branch of a blossoming tree, with the rising sun behind it. The design is stitched in dramatically contrasting colours – such contrast is very typical for an early summer morning!

Try working lines of Pekinese stitch parallel and close to each other. This is the way to turn a line stitch into filling. Detached buttonhole stitch opens a door to the amazing world of needlepoint techniques. To learn more of them is really worth doing!

SIZE

18 x 16cm (7 x 6¼in)

THREADS

DMC pearl cotton thread, size 8 (P8):

90 Variegated shades of yellow
51 Variegated pale yellow to carrot red
69 Variegated beige to brown
744 Yellow - pale
743 Yellow - medium

DMC pearl cotton thread, size 12 (P12):

644 Beige Grey - medium

DMC stranded cotton thread (SC):

90 Variegated shades of yellow
51 Variegated pale yellow to carrot red
725 Topaz
744 Yellow - pale
3078 Golden Yellow - very light
535 Ash Grey - very light
844 Beaver Grey - ultra dark
3021 Brown Grey - very dark

PATTERN NOTES

You have already seen the benefits of embellishing your design with variegated thread (see Snowdrop Swirl on page 78). Now learn a new trick: if you need two or three colours, but have only a ball of variegated pearl cotton, just cut this thread into sections showing the same colour, sorting them out into groups accordingly. Now use the proper colour - in this project to work fly stitch liana for the branch of the tree).

The instructions use some abbreviations of thread names, see page 24.

STITCHES USED

- Pekinese stitch, see page 106
- Buttonhole block shading, see page 106
- Battlement couching, see page 107
- Detached buttonhole – corded, see page 108
- Arrowhead stitch, see page 30
- Straight stitch, see page 30
- Outline stitch, see page 33
- Stem stitch (line or filling), see page 33
- Long-tailed daisy, see page 38
- Chain stitch, see page 39
- Fly stitch – liana, see page 49
- Fly stitch – leaf, see page 50
- Granitos, see page 51
- Buttonholed chain stitch, see page 53
- Buttonhole stitch (arranged in semi-circles), see page 56
- Seeding stitch, see page 60
- Split backstitch, see page 60
- Couching, see page 62
- Woven wheel, see page 64
- Fern stitch, see page 72
- Raised stem stitch, see page 74
- Pistil stitch, see page 77
- Woven bar leaf, see page 82
- Cretan stitch leaf, see page 84
- Ribbed wheel, see page 86
- Silk shading, see page 94
- Vermicelli stitch, see page 98

INSTRUCTIONS

Sun outline

1 Pekinese stitch: P8-90, laced with SC-90(6).

Daffodil

2 Buttonhole block shading SC-3078, 744, 725(2).

3 Daffodil tube: detached buttonhole – corded P8-743. The top part (in orange): pistil stitch and French knot P8-51.
Daffodil stem: outline stitch P8-743.

Bird

4 Pistil stitch and straight stitch P8-51.

5 Head: outline it in split backstitch P8-69. Beak: straight stitch SC-744(2).
Eye: stem stitch and French knot SC-844(1) and straight stitch SC-744(2).

6 Buttonhole block shading P8-51, 743, 744. Top part: silk shading in one colour SC-744(1).

7 Detached buttonhole – corded P8-69. Scallops: buttonhole semi-circles P8-69.

8 Three smaller feathers, central parts (left to right): fly stitch leaf (fly stitches are spaced) P8-51, fern stitch P8-69, backstitch P8-69. All the three feathers are outlined in chain stitch P8-51. The biggest feather: seeding stitch filling SC-90(1); outlined in Pekinese stitch: P8-90, laced with SC-90(6).

9 Top part of the wing: detached buttonhole – corded P8-69; scallops: buttonhole semi-circles P8-69. Bottom part of the wing: three lines of split backstitch P8-69, outlined in chain stitch P8-51.

10 Buttonhole semi-circles P8-69 (optional: outline one of them in stem stitch using a darker shade of P8-69). Legs: split backstitch P8-69. Feet: three daisy stitches P8-69.

11 Tail feathers (left to right). The first feather: Cretan stitch leaf P8-51, outlined in buttonholed chain stitch P12-644 and P8-51.
The second feather: pistil stitch and stem stitch SC-844(1).
The third feather: 'midrib' in pistil stitch placed in a line (one stitch over the other) P8-51; outlined in buttonholed chain stitch, P8-51.
Optional: one or two lines of stem stitch (to fill in the space) P8-743.
The fourth feather: backstitch for 'midrib', stem stitch to fill in the space, whipped split stitch to outline P12-644.

Branch

12 Fly stitch liana P12-644; P8-69; its bottom part outlined in stem stitch SC-844(1).

Working split backstitch first along the lines dividing areas of buttonhole block shading may help to get a smoother edge of buttonhole stitches (as it does to the edge of silk shading, see page 95).

Leaves

13 Smaller leaf: silk shading SC-535, 844, 3021(2;1).
Bigger leaf: laid work SC-535, 844, 3021(2;1).

14 Three smaller leaves: woven bar leaf SC-535; 3021(6;2).
Bigger leaf: seeding stitch (filling) SC-844(1), outlined in stem stitch SC-844(2).

15 Two Cretan stitch leaves SC-535, 844(2). Outline one of them in couching SC-3021(2;1).
Bottom leaf: seeding stitch SC-3021(1); outlined in stem stitch SC-844(2).

Hibiscus

16 First work the foundation of woven wheel (see page 64), only this time form it of six stitches. Using the properly-coloured sections of P8-69, work a small woven wheel (to cover one third of the length of foundation stitches); then finish with ribbed wheel. Note that the woven wheel technique requires an odd number of foundation stitches. Therefore, treat any two neighbouring stitches as one stitch when you weave – it will make no difference to the look, because the circle is so small. For the ribbed wheel, whip around each of the six stitches. Finally, work two or three circles in stem stitch P8-51 to make the flower centre nicely rounded.

17 Battlement couching P8-51 with tying stitches SC-744(1). Outline: one line of stem stitch P8-51 and then one line in outline stitch P12-644.

18 Vermicelli stitch SC-51(5), couched with SC-51(1).

Stem stitch P8-51 to outline the petals.

Crewel flower

19 Satin stitch SC-3078(6). covered with lattice P8-69 with tying stitches in SC-3078(1).

20 Silk shading SC-3078, 744, 90(1). The folded tip of the petal: detached buttonhole – corded P8-69.

21 Detached buttonhole – corded P8-743.

22 Buttonhole block shading P8-51, 743, 744.

23 'Ribs' of the flower cup (longer parts in beige brown): raised stem stitch P8-69. Flower cup (darker parts; intervals between 'ribs'): stem stitch filling P8-69.

24 Seeding stitch SC-90(1), outlined in couching P8-51, with tying stitches in SC-90(1). Cluster of pistils in dark brown: long-tailed daisy and straight stitch P8-69.

25 Battlement couching P8-51 with tying stitches SC-744(1). Outline: stem stitch P8-51.

Going further

The techniques mentioned in this section are to clarify some of the points stated earlier in this book and to further develop your skills. Ironically, I am going to mention a way of making knots where you can easily do without them, and another way of avoiding knots where it is alright to make them! The purpose of this is to show the variety of approaches in embroidery, and also to satisfy every desire, if possible.

INVISIBLE KNOT – TO FINISH STITCHING

Knots are generally unwelcome in embroidery: they come out big and messy, and therefore get in the way of your stitching. Here is a clever trick for making small and neat knots. It allows placing the knot level with the fabric, which makes the invisible knot technique a nice alternative to the regular ways of ending a thread (see page 23).

1 Turn your work to the back side. Unthread the needle and make a loose knot in the thread, close to the fabric surface.

2 Insert the needle, bringing it half-way through the fabric inside the loose loop.

3 Tighten up the thread around the needle: the needle 'guides' the knot down to the fabric surface!

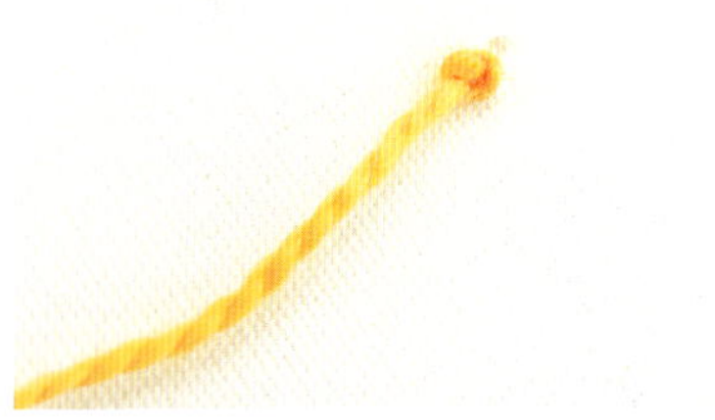

4 Remove the needle and tighten up the knot completely.

5 Trim off the excess thread. The knot comes out so small, it's almost invisible!

NO-KNOT WAY TO START STITCHING

This is just one of the ways to avoid knots in embroidery. Apply it if you wish to stitch without knots, or if you need to, for example while embroidering some garments or a napkin, where the back of the fabric is visible. (The example below features the buttonhole block shading technique, see page 106.)

1 Come up anywhere inside the area you are going to stitch, and leave a short thread tail on the back of the fabric. (Alternatively, you can go down, and leave a short thread tail on the right side of the fabric.)

2 Go down (alternatively: come up) close to the initial spot. Work a few very small stitches, each new stitch piercing the previous one. It is as if you were marching on the spot without moving forward.

3 The result is a tiny stitch on the right side of the fabric, which can easily be covered with the final stitching.

4 Come up at the beginning of the stitch line and trim off the short thread tail left in step 1: the anchorage is now secure enough to start the actual stitching.

CHAIN STITCH – REGULAR WAY OF WORKING

Compare this with reverse chain (see page 39) and choose to work it whichever way you prefer.

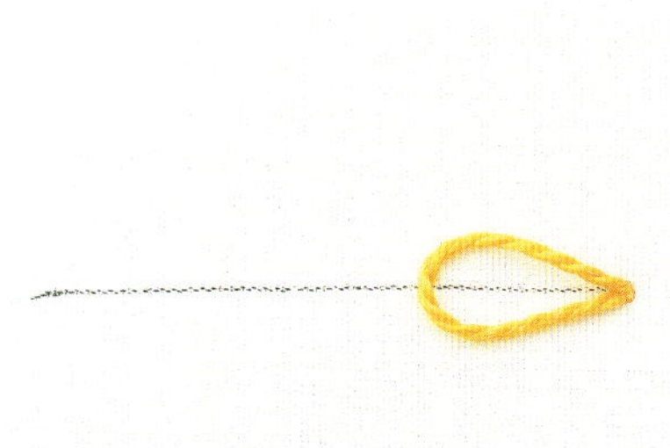

1 Work a loop at the beginning of the stitch line.

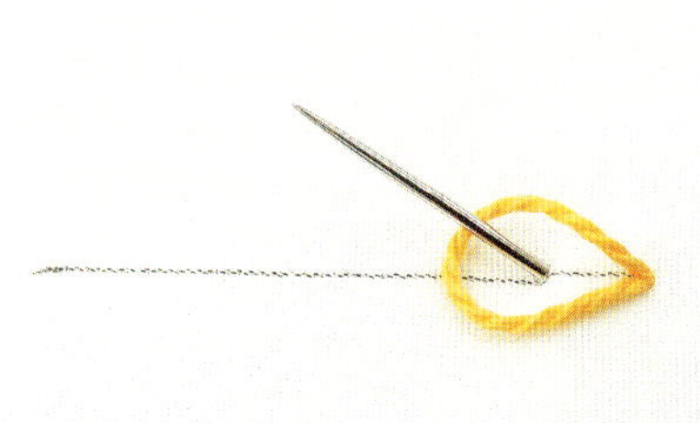

2 Bring the needle through the loop (shown halfway through the fabric for clarity).

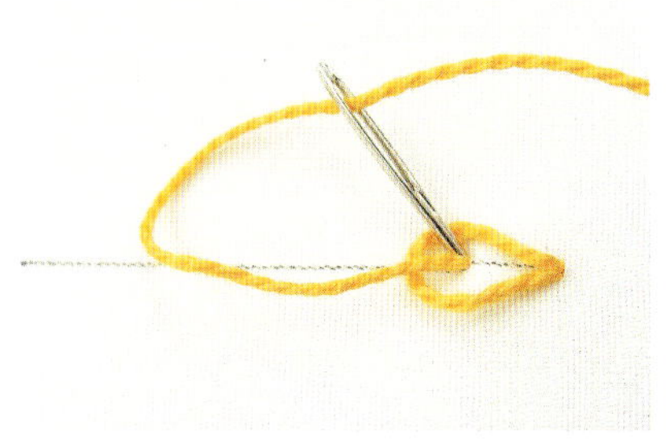

3 Go down close to where you came up, forming the second loop.

4 Continue working loops to the end of the stitch line. The sewing way of stitching is shown in the photograph for clarity. Work in the stabbing way, as in steps 2 and 3 (see page 21).

5 To anchor the last loop of the chain to the fabric, work a small tying stitch.

SPLIT STITCH – REGULAR WAY OF WORKING

There are two ways of working split stitch: the regular one (as shown below), and the one called split backstitch (see page 61). Despite the difference in names, both of them produce the same look of the finished stitch, so you can choose to follow whichever way you prefer.

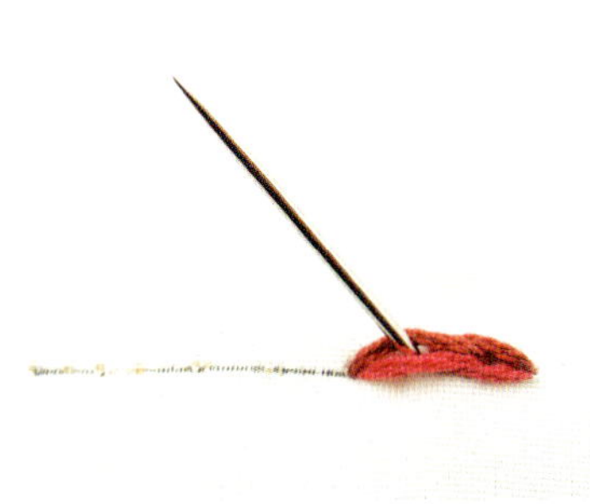

1 Come up at the beginning of the stitch line, work a straight stitch and bring the needle up through the straight stitch.

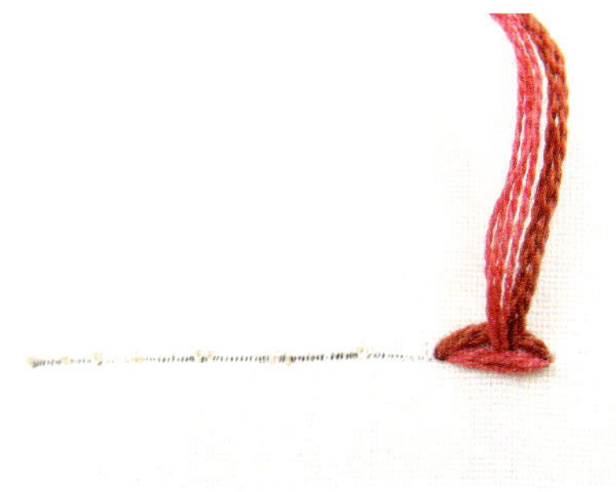

2 The result (shown in threads of two colours for clarity).

3 Go down to complete the second stitch.

4 To start a new stitch, always come up through the previous stitch. Bringing the needle through a stitch this way may be tricky, therefore an easier way is suggested – that is, split backstitch.

5 To complete a stitch, always go down a few millimetres away, further along the stitch line.

6 The finished stitch, shown in threads of two colours for clarity: work split stitch using a single thread.

Templates

All of the templates are shown at actual size. You can download extra copies of the templates for free from the Bookmarked Hub: www.bookmarkedhub.com Search for this book by title or ISBN: the files can be found under 'Book Extras'. Membership of the Bookmarked online community is free.

Gum Tree Leaves, page 34

Morning Glory, page 44

Crewel Poppy, page 54

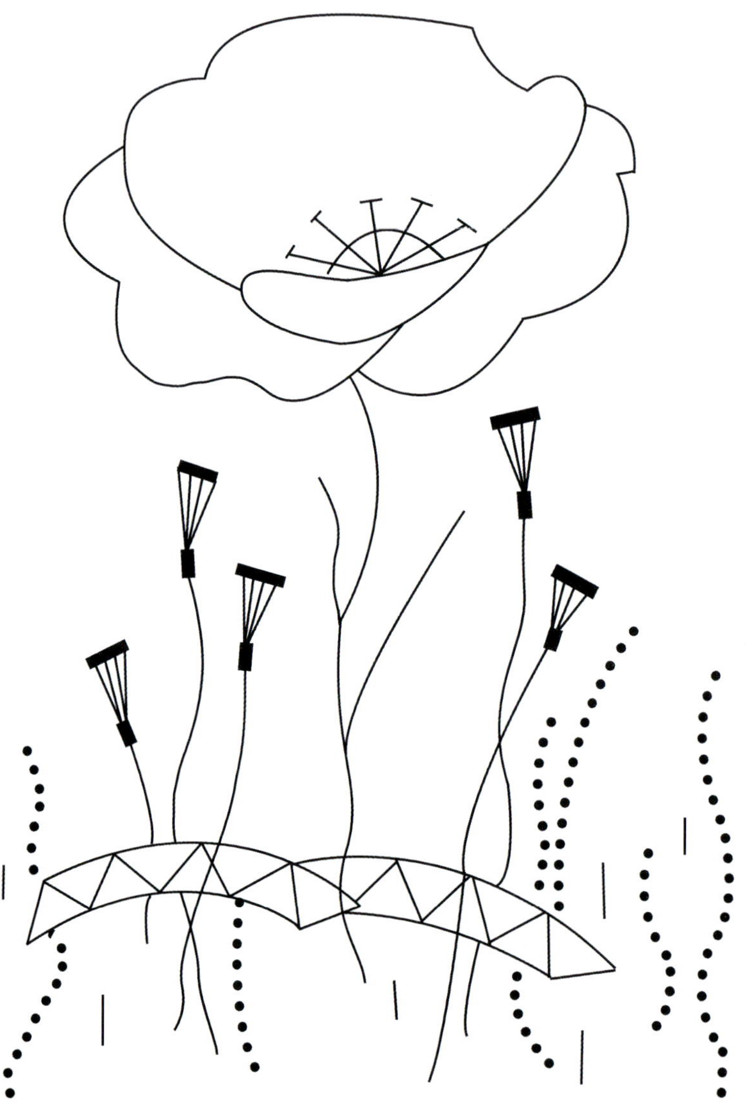

Floral Butterfly, page 66

Snowdrop Swirl, page 78

Peony, page 88

Fuchsia, page 100

Sunrise Singer, page 110

Stitch index